Charles Carroll of Carrollton

Fr. Charles P. Connor

CHARLES CARROLL OF CARROLLTON

American Revolutionary

EWTN PUBLISHING, INC.
Irondale, Alabama

Cover design: LUCAS Art & Design, Jenison, MI

Cover image: *Charles Carroll of Carrollton* by
Sir Joshua Reynold (Alamy EDYNY7)

EWTN Publishing, Inc.
5817 Old Leeds Road, Irondale, AL 35210

Distributed by Sophia Institute Press, Box 5284, Manchester, NH 03108.

paperback ISBN 978-1-68278-273-6
ebook ISBN 978-1-68278-274-3
Library of Congress Control Number: 2024936655

First printing

CONTENTS

FOREWORD BY CAMILLA CARROLL

I first met Fr. Connor at the rededication of our family chapel, St. Mary's, here at Doughoregan Manor. The chapel had not been in regular use for fifteen or twenty years and had not been refurbished since the early 1900s. When Fr. Connor first came here, every last inch of the house and chapel and everything in them had been repainted, repaired, cleaned, replaced, repointed, and otherwise restored. The chapel was the last big project. It was, therefore, a very emotional time for me and my family.

Although baptized Catholic, I was non-practicing all my life. As an adult with several dear friends in the clergy, I felt an irresistible pull toward the Church. At the rededication Mass, listening to Father's well-researched homily with its historical character, I knew that the decision to reestablish private Masses at the chapel was the right one.

Equally, if not more important, in my life has been the addition of Fr. Connor himself to the very short list of people I call my dear friends. He is not only an educated and talented author, but also a charming and magnetic man of God. I will never forget how wonderful I felt, even as a non-practicing Catholic, when he told me the work done here would be sending me straight to Heaven! It was the kind of thing he would say to me over and over again, and I knew he meant it.

I hope such personal memories are not out of place in a Foreword to a scholarly biography; somehow I think my fourth great-grandfather would not mind, especially since he knows I ended up joining the Church—that would be the most important thing for him, anyway. And Fr. Connor? He deserves every bit as much admiration as any of his books, and I am proud to give it to him.

Charles Carroll of Carrollton

Chapter 1

FROM WHENCE THEY CAME ... TO WHERE THEY WENT

Charles Carroll of Carrollton, revolutionary patriot, exemplary Catholic gentleman, and the sole member of his creed to sign the Declaration of Independence[1]—shortly before his death, confided to an old friend, Fr. Charles Constantine Pise:

> I have lived to my ninety-sixth year; I have enjoyed continued health, I have been blessed with great wealth, prosperity, and most of the good things which the world can bestow—public approbation, esteem, applause; but what I now look back on with the greatest satisfaction to myself is, that I have practiced the duties of my religion.[2]

From such, one may glean of patriotism and religious fervor. As Charles Carroll's life was drawing to a close in November 1832, he was the third generation of his family to live in, and

1 Mr. Carroll affixed his signature to the document in Philadelphia on August 2, 1776.

2 Kate Mason Rowland, *The Life of Charles Carroll of Carrollton, 1737–1832: With His Correspondence and Public Papers* (New York & London: G.P. Putnam's Sons, 1898), 11, 370.

exert significant influence over, first the Maryland Colony, then the new government of the United States. His own life began nearly four decades before the War of Independence and ended while Andrew Jackson, seventh President of the United States, was in office. Carroll was the last of the signers to die, the wealthiest man in the colonies and the new republic, and clung tenaciously to the Faith of his forebearers his entire life. To write a biography of such a venerable American icon involves, of necessity, a careful scrutiny of those who preceded him, the land from which they came, and the new world they entered.

As their surname suggests, Ireland was the ancestral land of the Carrolls, specifically, Ballymooney in County Offaly, in the province of Leinster, in the Irish midlands. The family's lives and fortunes were interwoven with seventeenth-century British and Irish affairs and involved dealings, in one way or another, with the four Stuart monarchs who reigned from 1603 until 1688. No sooner had James I assumed the throne that effects were felt in their country of origin.[3] One historical account notes that:

> The government at once seized the opportunity to assume control of the resources which had made possible resistance to English rule in Ulster. Much of the land in the province was taken from the Irish and granted in small amounts to English and Scots settlers. In this

[3] James I reigned from 1603 to 1625. He began the period of the Stuarts, which, with the exception of the decade of the Protectorate and Commonwealth (1649–1659) led by Oliver Cromwell, was to last until the Glorious Revolution of 1688, which witnessed the overthrow of the Stuarts and the assumption of power by William and Mary, sealing, as it were, Protestant domination of the Empire.

> way, a vigorous new Protestant community was created as a counterbalance to the influence of the Catholic Irish. At the same time, the steady increase in English authority throughout Ireland ... seriously diminished the influence and endangered the property of the "old English"—those Catholic descendants of earlier settlers who had remained loyal to the English Crown, but whose Catholicism the Crown increasingly distrusted.[4]

Landlords had, in effect, become royal vassals. James I "seized the O'Carroll family lands under this policy in 1615," and when the O'Carrolls some decades later joined a rebellion, James's successor Charles I "degraded them further, to tenants at pleasure,"[5] though Catholics, at times, had been seriously persecuted under the monarch's predecessor, Elizabeth I.

> The rigor of their execution was softened by the fact that ... James I became financially dependent on recusancy fines, the penalties Catholics had to pay for not attending Anglican services. To eliminate the Catholic community entirely would have killed the goose that was laying the golden eggs. Nevertheless, periodic outbreaks of anti-Catholic hysteria resulted in new hangings, drawings, and quarterings until the public rage was satisfied.[6]

Such rage had been exacerbated early in James's tenure by the famous Gunpowder Plot of 1605. The circulated story was that a Catholic coup d'etat would take place after the

4 Victor Meally (ed.), *Encyclopedia of Ireland* (Dublin: Allen Figgis & Co. Limited), 88. The term *Ulster* used here designates the province comprising the nine northernmost counties in Ireland.

5 Scott McDermott, *Charles Carroll of Carrollton: Faithful Revolutionary* (New York: Scepter Publishers, 1968), 17.

6 Ibid., 18.

House of Lords had been blown up on the opening day of the parliamentary session, when the king and queen would be present. A soldier, Guy Fawkes, was to be responsible for placing explosives in a vault after an underground passage had been dug from a nearby cellar. Fawkes apparently had brought in thirty-six barrels of gunpowder, but the plan failed when an anonymous message was sent to one of the members of the Lords, advising him not to attend. On the evening of November 4, 1605, Fawkes was apprehended with the barrels of gunpowder and ultimately tried and hanged. Seven others associated with him met the same fate, and the public mood only intensified against Catholics.[7]

In 1625, Charles I assumed the throne following the death of his father, James. His queen, Henrietta Maria, sister of the French King Louis XIII, was the one for whom the Colony of Maryland was named. Charles's very stormy relations with Parliament over nearly a quarter-century led somewhat easily to his demise. For the last eleven years of his reign, he refused to even convene Parliament, and in 1649 was placed on trial for high treason—the principal cause, it was argued, for England's troubles. He refused to plead, arguing that a king could not legally be tried in Westminster Hall by members of Parliament. He was eventually beheaded following the lengthy period remembered as the English Civil

7 Curiously, Guy Fawkes Day became somewhat of an anti-Catholic celebration each year on the anniversary of the Gunpowder Plot's failure, both in England and later in the American colonies. General George Washington gave strict orders to his soldiers in the Revolutionary War not to observe this date with any kind of public display. This, especially in light of the assistance of France during the American Revolution.

War, and the Puritan ascendancy of Oliver Cromwell would seize power for the next decade.

Charles I played a significant role in the Carroll saga, since it was he who granted a proprietary charter to George Calvert to establish the Palatinate of Maryland. Born in 1579 or 1580 in Yorkshire, Calvert, as a young man, remembered his parents being told of the expectation to conform to the established church. When George was no more than thirteen, secular authorities compelled him to conform as well, underscoring the fact that he was a practicing member of the Anglican Church for more than three decades.

After graduation from Oxford, he studied law at Lincoln's Inn, took an extensive stay on the Continent, returned and placed himself under the political mentorship of Sir Robert Cecil, the "principal manipulator of the dynastic change in 1603."[8] Calvert was introduced to court politics and to many of the luminaries of the age. He married in the Anglican Church, rose to clerk of the Privy Council, and then to the position of courtier in the service of King James. One of the occupational hazards of his loyalty was his staunch support for the policy of reconciliation with Spain that King James favored; contemporary observers began to wonder if he had reverted to the Faith of his Baptism—it was not difficult to be a Catholic and support James's Spanish policy but just about impossible to be a zealous Protestant and do so. As time went on, "it caused Calvert to be labeled, like his monarch, as worryingly pro-Catholic."[9]

8 John D. Krugler, *English and Catholic: The Lords Baltimore in the Seventeenth Century* (Baltimore: Johns Hopkins University Press, 2004), 10.

9 Charles P. Connor, *Pioneer Priests and Makeshift Altars: A History of Catholicism in the Thirteen Colonies* (Irondale: EWTN Publishing, 2017), 56.

> Why did Calvert abandon his long-standing conformity? No one individual ... was responsible for his decision. Rather, it was the culmination of many influences ... Contemporary descriptions indicate that the events that led to his resignation as secretary depressed him and led to a period of introspection and reassessment. He realized for the first time in two decades that he faced the prospect of exclusion from the nexus of power. He also came to see that the loss of office relieved him of a burden. It allowed him to resolve his conflicted religious loyalties.[10]

A somewhat more admiring commentator noted:

> The single fact of his public conversion to Catholicism in 1624 when every earthly inducement would prompt him to remain an Anglican, proves as nothing else could the depth of the man's sincerity and moral rectitude. In general historians have not been conspicuous in their praise and credit to Calvert for setting on foot what was for that time an altogether unprecedented experiment in religious freedom.[11]

The unprecedented experiment referenced was none other than the charter for the Palatinate of Maryland granted Calvert by Charles I. The king's wife, Henrietta Maria, was a devout Catholic who had great concern for her coreligionists in Britain, and so the Calverts continued to receive the favor of the Crown. The colonial charter given George Calvert contained a "Bishop of Durham" clause, similar in its sweeping breath of political power to that enjoyed by the

[10] Krugler, 73–74. For more particular arguments bantered about by historians, see Connor, *Pioneer Priests*, 58.

[11] John Tracy Ellis, *Catholics in Colonial America* (Baltimore: Helicon Press, 1965), 325.

Palatinate of Durham, an ancient city on the English-Scottish border. George Calvert died before his American grant could be settled, and so it passed to his son Cecil. In turn, it was Cecil's brother Leonard who actually made the voyage to Maryland, arriving at St. Clement's Island with colonists, Jesuits, and indentured servants on March 25, 1634, where the first Mass was offered by Fr. Andrew White, S.J.

As to Lord Baltimore's efforts at colonization:

> His greatest success would come from those who saw the opportunity for political power and social status. Generally, these were the second and third sons of prosperous British families who knew they would not inherit the whole of the family fortune. Of these, the majority were Catholics of the gentry class—and usually had long ties to the Calvert family. Their religion generally stood in the way of any type of advancement in England, and their willingness to make the voyage to the New World became stronger the more they eyed their current reality.[12]

The Maryland Colony was established with the arrival of the ships the *Ark* and the *Dove*, and it would be over one-half century before the first Carroll settler would arrive in the then-established city of Annapolis. Calvert's generous grant of religious toleration to all those arriving in the colony was short lived. By 1649, Charles I was dead, Oliver Cromwell and the Puritans had taken strong political control in England, and the result in colonial Maryland was a swift repeal of the Act of Toleration in 1654.

> That none who profess and exercise the Popish religion, commonly known by the name of Roman Catholic, can be protected in this province, by the laws of England,

[12] Connor, 64.

> formerly established and yet unrepealed ... but are to be restrained from the exercise thereof. Therefore all and every person or persons concerned in the law aforesaid are required to take notice. Such as profess faith in God by Jesus Christ, though differing in judgement from the doctrine, worship and discipline publicly held forth, shall not be restrained from, but shall be protected in the profession of the faith and exercise of their religion, so as they abuse not this liberty to the injury of others, the disturbance of the public peace on their part, provided that this liberty be not extended to popery or prelacy nor to such as under the profession of Christ hold forth and practice licentiousness.[13]

It was not long before Protestants had achieved an electoral majority and political control in Maryland. The colony had suffered through an unsuccessful naval assault by William Claiborne of Virginia, who, joining forces with a Puritan, Richard Ingle, invaded Maryland and seized control. The period became known as the "plundering time," and, though Claiborne achieved brief success, Cromwell eventually restored political control to the proprietor. Lord Baltimore, as might well be expected, pardoned the insurgents, and eventually restored the Act of Toleration. In England, Cromwell was quickly losing control, and after his death, there was a gradual drift toward anarchy, and in 1660, Parliament opened negotiations with Charles II to restore the Stuart monarchy. The son of Charles I, he had been in political exile for nearly eleven years, and, upon assuming the throne, his reign seemed to be dominated by religion. "He was by nature tolerant," one historical account relates,

[13] Francis X. Curran, S.J., *Catholics in Colonial Law* (Chicago: Loyola University Press, 1963), 30–31.

"partly because he wished to heal national wounds, and partly because the influence of his years in exile predisposed him to freedom for Roman Catholics."[14]

This being so, Catholics seemed to fare little better under Charles II, partly because of a 1678 event known as the Titus Oates Plot. Rumors began to be circulated in London of a fictitious Jesuit plot to murder Charles and replace him with his brother James, Duke of York, a Roman Catholic.

> Its existence was dreamt up by Titus Oates (1648–1705), a failed Anglican clergyman who had also partly trained as a Catholic priest in Spain and France. His experience gave his story just enough authentic detail for it to be believed in an age when religion was the tinderbox of politics. He was treated with high honor as the saviour of the nation and given a pension. His false accusations sent some 35 people to their deaths before the deception was realized. Convicted for perjury in 1685, his own punishment was only flogging and imprisonment.[15]

Anti-Catholic hysteria was marked in Britain, so much so that many favored a legal prohibition against the Duke of York's right to succeed his brother upon his death. Such did not happen, and even Charles II converted to Catholicism shortly before his death. James II assumed the throne in 1685, but opposition was so strong from the outset, that one may trace the division between the Whig and Tory political parties to the struggle among the monarch's friends and enemies. In 1687, the king suspended the laws which prevented Roman Catholics and Nonconformists from holding

[14] Bamber Gascoigne, *Encyclopedia of Britain* (Basingstoke: Macmillan Publishers, Ltd., 1993), 127.

[15] Ibid., 500.

political office. James had converted to Catholicism in 1669, though he continued attending Anglican services for another seven years. His marriage to the Catholic Mary of Modena, and her giving birth to a male heir, furthered the fear of another Catholic coming to the throne. This, among other factors, would result in the Glorious Revolution of 1688, in which a large number of James's Protestant officers defected to William III, who, with his wife Mary, began the permanent Protestant ascendancy in England following the decisive Battle of the Boyne, when any and all hopes of James reassuming the throne were dashed. He would ultimately die in France, but for two more generations his most ardent Jacobite followers remained intensely loyal to his descendants.

It was against this political landscape that a young man from Ireland left his native shores to settle in the Maryland colony, first at St. Mary's City in southern Maryland, where the center of colonial government was located, then in the newly emerging city on the Severn River, Annapolis. He has been described by one biographer as "the kind of person who never gets old and tired, no matter how long he may live; who cannot be thought about as dead, no matter how long ago he may have died. He was always younger than his more illustrious, more dignified grandson."[16] The grandson, the subject of this biography, is Charles Carroll of Carrollton; to his colorful grandfather historians have traditionally given the name Charles Carroll the Settler.[17]

[16] Ellen Hart Smith, *Charles Carroll of Carrollton* (New York: Russell & Russell, 1942), 4.

[17] He is also referred to as Charles Carroll the Attorney General because he carried with him Lord Baltimore's commission for that office for the Province of Maryland.

The Settler—son of Daniel Carroll of Aghagurty (and Litterluna), the descendant of an earlier Daniel Carroll of Ballymooney—was born in 1661 just after the Stuart restoration, which followed Cromwell's devastating attempt to stamp out Catholic Ireland. Through the auspices of a relative, Richard Grace, a fiercely loyal partisan of the Stuarts whose loyalty had financially served him very well, Carroll obtained an excellent education in France at the University of Douai. The school had begun in the 1560s and remained a center of education for English (and Irish) Catholics until the period of the French Revolution in the late eighteenth century. Located in the town was the English College established by Cardinal William Allen for the training of young men for the Catholic priesthood, as well as Irish and Scottish colleges, along with the religious houses of the Benedictines, Franciscans, and Jesuits. Carroll himself was educated there as a lawyer and went to England briefly to pursue the first steps in a legal career. There seems little doubt that the persecutions leveled at Catholics in the realm were the primary inducement for him to leave and make the journey to Maryland, where he could live life, and hopefully practice his Catholic Faith with no interference.

Two weeks after his arrival, James II was deposed and the Glorious Revolution sealed the Protestant ascendancy under William III. Within a brief few years, the proprietary government of the Calverts—the Lords Baltimore—was toppled, and Maryland became a royal colony, which it would remain until 1715. Baltimore was, however, "secured in the possession of his private rights, his ownership of the soil and the vacant lands, the quit-rents, port dues, and one half of the tobacco duties."[18] Displaying what seemed a boundless optimism, the

[18] Rowland, 1, 4.

Settler now changed the official family motto to *Ubicumque cum Libertate,* "anywhere so long as there be freedom." Reflecting two generations later, his grandson, Charles Carroll of Carrollton wrote, "My grandfather was destined to experience even in the asylum he had selected, the evils of that religious persecution from which he had so recently fled."[19]

How then did the Settler achieve the social prominence, and especially the financial success, that characterizes his life? One historical account attributes it to marrying well. The Settler first succeeded by:

> contracting a marriage in November 1689 with a wealthy widow named Martha Ridgley Underwood. Several years his senior and the mother of four young children, Martha had come to Maryland as an indentured servant, but by 1671 she had married the man to whom she was bound—Robert Ridgely, a Protestant, prominent attorney, and holder of several provincial offices. Upon Ridgely's death in 1681, Martha inherited a sizeable estate consisting of two plantations ... along with all of her husband's personal property, including household goods, plates, servants and slaves, livestock, and debts owed to him, totaling in value five hundred pounds. Sometime after 1683 Martha Ridgely married Anthony Underwood, a former bound servant and law clerk of her first husband. A prime example of the fluid socioeconomic conditions that still prevailed in Maryland, Underwood, who had some legal training and had worked as a clerk in England, began to practice law upon completing his servitude and by March 1682 had gained admission to the provincial court. In 1685 ... he secured the position of alderman in St. Mary's City, and

[19] McDermott, 25.

> the following year he gained a seat in the lower house of the Maryland Assembly. When his upward career ended with his death at age thirty in 1689 Underwood left a personal estate—worth nearly 550 [pounds] sterling and about two thousand acres of land. Into this convenient breech stepped the enterprising and ambitious Charles Carroll the Settler, who happened to be the executor of Anthony Underwood's estate. On November 9, 1689, no more than six months after Underwood's demise, Carroll wed the well-provisioned Martha . . . The union was short. In November 1690, Martha Ridgely Underwood Carroll, who had borne Anthony Underwood no children, died in childbirth, followed three days later by the infant son who had been christened Anthony . . . Carroll, barely two years after his arrival in Maryland, and despite the obstacles resulting from the Glorious Revolution, had by means of his marriage positioned himself to take immediate advantage of Maryland's agricultural and mercantile opportunities.[20]

More success was to follow. Despite the many anti-Catholic restrictions one found in colonial Maryland, Carroll was able to offer shrewd and very helpful legal advice to Charles Calvert, third Lord Baltimore as well as his cousin, Colonel Henry Darnall, who oversaw Lord Baltimore's interests in Maryland.

> Once again Carroll had positioned himself to the utmost advantage, and in February 1693/4 he moved decisively to consolidate his gains by marrying the Colonel's fifteen-year-old daughter, Mary, a girl less than half his age. The opportunities this alliance brought Carroll

20 Ronald Hoffman and Sally D. Mason, *Princes of Ireland, Planters of Maryland: A Carroll Saga, 1500–1782* (Chapel Hill: University of North Carolina Press, 2000), 64–65.

> can scarcely be exaggerated. Until the overthrow of the proprietary government, Darnall sat on the council, the colony's most powerful political body, served on the board of deputy governors and the land council, was the proprietor's rent roll keeper, and held the two extremely lucrative offices of Lord Baltimore's agent and receiver general, and keeper of the great seal. Most significantly, Darnall, though deprived, like all non- conforming Catholics, of his political posts after 1689, had retained all his positions within the proprietor's private establishment, and the power and wealth that continued to flow from these posts made him indisputably one of the colony's dominant personalities.[21]

Finally,

> Carroll had hardly recited his wedding vows, when his fortunes took still another turn for the better. Darnall bestowed on his new son-in-law two Prince George's County tracts totaling 1,381 acres. Far more important, when Maryland's land office reopened in May, 1694, the colonel appointed Carroll clerk, a position that carried a salary of approximately 100 [pounds] a year and placed him at the center of all land transactions.[22]

The Settler's career "exemplifies the classic pattern of broadly diversified Chesapeake entrepreneurs who built fortunes by combining strategic marriages with the activities of a planter, banker, lawyer, merchant, and proprietary officeholder."[23]

One facet of the Settler's personality was his decided Irishness. It came to the forefront in his strongly vocal

[21] Ibid., 67.
[22] Ibid., 70.
[23] Ibid.

criticisms of the colonial government, especially after the fall of James II from power, and the Glorious Revolution cementing Protestantism throughout the realm, and just as stridently in the American colonies. The fact of the Church of England, small in numbers though it was, becoming the established church upon Maryland becoming a royal colony only added to his discontent. Two brief jail stays were the result of his protests, but, as in so many other areas, the Settler fought back, and always seemed to land on his feet.

The Settler always kept his Irish identity and made it his project to bring as many Irish to Maryland as possible, in spite of taxes designed to discourage Irish immigration. He demanded that his son, Carroll of Annapolis, style himself "Marylando-Hibernus" while studying in France. Carroll of Annapolis, in turn, lectured his own son about "the duty all Irishmen owe to the glory and honor of their country." The third Charles Carroll, however, chafed at his father's Irish victim-consciousness. Declining to visit Ireland, Carrollton mused, "How unavailing to remember what we cannot revenge! How melancholy to behold the ancient, noble, and once flourishing families reduced to beggary!"[24]

It was not long before the Maryland Protestant ascendency sought to force its will on Catholics—those who had insisted on religious toleration for Christians who settled the colony. The Colonial Assembly was unsuccessful in making

[24] McDermott, 27. The third Carroll referred to here is, of course, the Signer. Intermarriage with a number of English Catholic families by both his father and grandfather had insured that Charles Carroll of Carrollton had as much English blood as Irish, not to mention the distance from the family's Irish origins time can produce.

attendance at Anglican services compulsory. King William did not wish to grant all the rights of Englishmen to colonials, and twice vetoed acts of the Assembly which declared all English laws to be in effect in Maryland. The legislators then decided to take matters into their own hands and passed one of the most anti-Catholic pieces of legislation up to that point. In 1704, the "Act to Prevent the Growth of Popery within this Province" was unique in several ways:

> Whatsoever Popish bishop, priest or Jesuit shall baptize any child or children other than such who have Popish parents, or shall say Mass or exercise the function of a Popish bishop or priest within this province, or shall endeavor to persuade any of her majesty's liege people to embrace and be reconciled to the Church of Rome and shall be thereof legally convict, shall forfeit the sum of fifty pounds sterling for every such offence ... and shall also suffer six months' imprisonment of his or their body or bodies without bail or mainprise ... if any Popish bishop, priest or Jesuit after such conviction aforesaid shall say Mass or exercise any other part of the office or function of a Popish bishop or priest within this province, or if any Papist or person making profession of the Popish religion shall keep school ... such person or persons ... shall upon such conviction be transported out of this province to the Kingdom of England together with his conviction, in order to his suffering such pains and penalties as are provided by the statute made in the 11th and 12th year of the reign of his late Majesty, King William the Third, entitled *An Act* for the further prevention of the growth of Popery.[25]

[25] Cited in Curran, 82.

Protests over the legislation became so vocal that the governor and the Maryland Assembly temporarily allowed for the saying of Masses, provided they were conducted in private homes. It was understood that this grace period was to extend for eighteen months, and when it was nearing its conclusion, Maryland Catholics again petitioned that it be extended. At first, the legislature rejected the petition but eventually came around to extend it for another year. By 1706, Catholics were beginning to see a bit of light when the British Parliament ruled that the 1704 legislation be permanently suspended. In another thirteen years, it would be totally repealed.

Through the years, Carroll the Settler had been accumulating great wealth, and great estates in various locales in the colony. He named his manors after ancient family estates in Ireland—Ely O'Carroll, Litterluna, and "his favorite manor he called, with characteristic grandiloquence, Doughoregan, or House of Kings."[26] All cannot be judged by the fortunes of one man, however, nor even by a small number of affluent English Catholics who had settled the colony. The years following the toppling of James II were understandably not to augur well for Catholics, and as one Protestant monarch succeeded the other in England, colonial legislatures up and down the Atlantic seaboard were emboldened to pass all sorts of restrictive measures against members of the Church of Rome. William III had succeeded James II (his father-in-law), and

[26] Smith, 15. Doughoregan Manor is still in the possession of the Carroll family. It is located close to Ellicott City and just across the road from the site of the first St. Charles College/Seminary for the training of priests. It was Charles Carroll of Carrollton who gave the original land for the seminary's building, and seminary faculty priests regularly celebrated Mass in the Manor Chapel for Carroll and his family members.

since a Catholic heir had been born to James and his wife, Parliament was invited to Britain to seize the Crown. William and his wife ruled jointly until her death in 1694, and he alone until his own death in 1702. In turn, he was succeeded by his sister-in-law Anne, the second daughter of James II and Anne Hyde. A glimpse into her priorities is telling:

> At home, her policies were guided largely by her devotion to the Anglican Church, a commitment which had caused her to welcome the Protestant William III when he replaced her Roman Catholic father on the throne. One of her most lasting acts as queen was to use the Crown revenue from the Church (originally taxes paid to the pope appropriated by Henry VIII) to increase the livings of the poorer parish clergy.[27]

With Anne's death in 1714 came the end of the Stuart monarchy, and the rule of the various Georges of Hanover, the first of whom claimed the throne through his mother, who had been a granddaughter of James I. George I was succeeded by his son George II in 1727, who was succeeded by his grandson George III in 1760—the reigning monarch during the American Revolution and the winning of American Independence. A series of legislative enactments in Maryland early in the reign of George I made even easier the defection of Benedict Leonard Calvert, fourth Lord Baltimore, to the Anglican Church. Calvert was divorced and had accumulated huge expenses maintaining his ex-wife. He hoped by conforming to the established church that life would be substantially easier. He would not live long enough for that question to be answered; he died in 1716, and was succeeded by his son, Charles Calvert, now

[27] Gascoigne, 27.

fifth Lord Baltimore. Charles had been educated by the Jesuits in French Flanders and as a young man had expressed the view that he would rather "lose his estate than his Catholic religion."

Now reconciled to the Church of England, the young lord assumed the full proprietorship on December 15, 1715. This meant that the Settler lost the Attorney Generalship, because the proprietor's private estate once again became part of the public sector, and Catholics were barred from public office.[28]

The background is important to understand the Maryland legislation which followed. In 1715, women in the colony were advised that upon the death of any Protestant gentleman who left a widow and children, should that widow subsequently remarry a Catholic, or be of the Catholic religion herself, "it shall and may be lawful for His Majesty's governor and council within this province upon application to them made to remove such child or children out of the custody of such parents and place them where they may be securely educated in the Protestant religion."[29] A year later, Catholics were effectively excluded from political office by the requirement to take a specific oath, the mere wording of which intended to deter them:

> I, (name), do swear that I do from my heart abhor, detest and abjure, as impious and heretical, that damnable doctrine and position, that princes excommunicated or deprived by the Pope, or any authority of the See of Rome, may be deposed or murdered by their subjects, or any other whatsoever. And I do declare,

[28] McDermott, 29.
[29] Cited in Curran, 93.

> that no foreign prince, person, prelate, state or potentiate, has, or ought to have, any jurisdiction, power, superiority, pre-eminence, or authority, ecclesiastical or spiritual, within the Kingdom of Great Britain, or any of the dominions thereto belonging. So help me God.[30]

Finally, because of the substantial number of Irish servants coming to Maryland to work in the homes of wealthy English Catholics, or wherever they could secure employment in the colony, "an additional sum of twenty shillings current money, over and above the twenty shillings sterling per poll imposed by a former act of assembly, for every Irish servant so imported."[31]

In the midst of all this, the Settler had gone to England to lobby for the rights of Catholics. Some historians believe his action so angered the colonial powers that these pieces of legislation were a rebuttal. His trip ended, it would appear, in a personal rebuttal which had far-reaching effects, and in the aftermath of these events:

> Numerous Maryland Catholics conformed to the Church of England. Those who remained Catholic, it has been claimed, were forbidden to walk in front of the state house, presumably for fear of a second

30 Ibid., 94. Two years later, further specifications were added with an act declaring that "all professed Papists whatsoever be (and are hereby declared) uncapable of giving their vote in any election of a delegate or delegates within this province, either for counties, cities, or boroughs, unless they first qualify themselves for so doing, by taking the several oaths appointed to be taken by an act of assembly of this province, entitled an act for the better security of the peace and safety of his Lordship's government and the Protestant interest within this province, and subscribe the oath of abjuration and declaration therein mentioned." Ibid., 96.

31 Ibid., 92.

> Gunpowder Plot. Annapolis tradition holds that Catholics had to wear swords to guarantee their safety.[32]

Mary Darnall bore the Settler ten children, of whom five lived to adulthood. Of those five, three were boys: Henry, Daniel, and Charles of Annapolis. Henry, born in 1697, would die quite a young man, on a return voyage from French Flanders where he was enrolled in a Jesuit school; Daniel, born in 1707, married Ann, daughter of Notley Rozier of Notley Hall, Maryland, and headed a branch of the family often called the Carrolls of Duddington, named for their estate in Prince George's County, upon which now stands the capital building of the United States. Charles of Annapolis would become the father of the Signer of the Declaration of Independence. One of the family's leading biographical teams has summed up the Settler's life:

> On July 1, 1720, Charles Carroll died leaving his coreligionists and his descendants an ironic and compelling legacy. To the former, Carroll left the political disabilities that would bind Maryland Catholics until the coming of the American Revolution. To his heirs he bequeathed the most substantial estate ever created in Maryland to that time, a fierce tribal loyalty, and a tenacious memory. The Settler's personality and perception of the world bore the indelible imprint of the ruthless struggle over land and culture waged by his Gaelic forebearers and the English and Irish Protestants intent on displacing them. Raised in the crucible of that conflict, he had traveled to Maryland on an inflexible quest to reconstitute the Carroll fortune and lay the foundations of a renewed dynasty.[33]

32 McDermott, 30.
33 Hoffman and Mason, 96–97.

Yet, at the same time:

> Because of the Carrolls' unbending adherence to their Catholic faith, their story provides a unique perspective on early America. Despite great wealth, their religion cast them as outsiders, persons stripped of all political and most civil rights by Protestant authority ... Maryland's wealthy Catholics—ten of the colony's twenty largest fortunes belonged to people derisively known as "papists"—found life far more insecure. Although Catholics constituted less than ten percent of Maryland's population, the economic success of the Catholic gentry loomed disproportionally in the consciousness of the colony's non-Catholic majority and periodically became a focus for both local discontent and official jealously. Nor did the legal system protect them; indeed, it imperiled their existence. Since the enactment of the Elizabethan penal codes during the last half of the sixteenth century, English law had been used to destroy Catholic wealth ... Spared from the threat of this legislation until 1689, Maryland's Catholics lived from that date until the eve of the American Revolution with the very real possibility that their lands would be taken. For those economically menaced and politically marginalized families, Chesapeake society assumed a capricious and arbitrary reality that separated their experience from that of the broader, occasionally militant Protestant gentry.

As a result:

> The Carrolls' position as Catholic outsiders in Protestant Maryland and their conscious memory of their family's long, bitter, and ultimately futile struggle against conquest and dispossession in Ireland provide more than a different perspective on early American society.[34]

[34] Ibid., xx.

A closer look at how that society came to be is necessary to any understanding of the Carroll family saga through the generations, and especially of the world that molded Charles Carroll of Carrollton and sharply defined his patriotism.

It has been observed by at least one commentator on the origins of North America that contemplation never crossed the ocean. The meaning of this stresses the mentality of those who left Europe for newer shores. It was a departure from what was viewed as the decadence of European civilization, and most important, a departure from the ancient religious creed which claimed the adherence of their ancestors, a creed from which the overwhelming majority of a newer generation had been freed by the Protestant Reformation of the sixteenth century. The American was to be a totally new creation, fully imbued with a strong Calvinistic theology, and to a lesser degree, Lutheran; even the break of Henry VIII in England was seen to smack too much of the vestiges of Romanism to suit many new arrivals.

It was the meeting of the alien yet conquerable land with English-speaking Protestants. Since the crossing of the ocean, we have been Europeans who were not Europeans. But the Europeanness which remained for us was of a special kind because Calvinist Protestantism was itself a break in Europe—a turning away from the Greeks in the name of what was found in the Bible.[35]

It is difficult to exaggerate the harm that was inflicted on the centuries of Christian culture in Europe by the Reformation. Religious and civil war followed on so many parts of the

[35] George Grant, *Technology and Empire: Perspectives on North America* (Toronto: House of Anansi, 1969), 19.

Continent, and any sort of reconciliation had so passed from men's minds as to appear impossible. Luther and Calvin were the two most prominent theological reformers, and though both influenced American culture, Calvin by far had the most devastating effect. He was born in Noyon in Picardy, remarkably well educated in Paris, Bourges, and Orleans, and emerged from this a lawyer, classical scholar, and theologian. At some point in the 1520s he became a Protestant, though practically nothing is known of the particulars of his change of belief. He has been described as the antithesis of Luther, seemingly never experiencing "doubt or fears or psychological crises" but rather followed "one undeviating line with absolute conviction and certitude; an austere, reserved, self-controlled man with a powerful and logical mind and a strong sense of authority and order."[36] He is best remembered for his *Institutes of the Christian Religion,* published in 1536, likely in Basel, Switzerland. This work would dominate the Protestant mind for the next two centuries, laying out as it did Calvin's blueprint for church organization and government, as well as the theological principles upon which such blueprint was based.

> From a purely doctrinal standpoint the differences between Luther and Calvin are extremely small. Both of them base their systems on the central dogma of justification by faith alone; and both emphasize the all-importance of the doctrine of predestination and the necessity for the believer to possess a consciousness of his justification; both make the Bible the only rule of Faith to the exclusion of all ecclesiastical tradition; both denounce the Papacy as anti-Christ; and both conceive the true Catholic Church as an

[36] Christopher Dawson, *The Dividing of Christendom* (New York: Sheed and Ward, 1965), 127–128.

> invisible society of elected saints. Thus the margin of theological difference is very narrow, and it was easy in theory to entertain the notion of a common Protestantism. Nevertheless the spirit of the two systems differed as widely as the spirit of the two Reformers. The theology of Luther is always Christocentric, whereas that of the *Institutes* is theocentric and centers on the mystery of the Divine Decrees. But, above all, it is in the practical working out of the two systems . . . that the differences are most extreme. Luther's Reformation was, from the beginning, decreed against the Church as an embodiment of spiritual power . . . Calvin, on the other hand, was determined to uphold and defend the autonomy of the Church . . . In his view the first essential of a reformed Church was to be reformed in discipline and morals. And therefore he brought back the spiritual authority and law of the Church in an even more drastic form than that of the Catholic Church.[37]

This was accomplished in an association of the clergy with the laity, the consistory, which included the four orders of teacher, pastor, elder, and deacon—all of whom, in their respective spheres—strictly controlled and supervised the faith and morals of the congregation. Wherever the Calvinist system triumphed, be it among French Huguenots, Scotch Presbyterians, or English and American Puritans, there was to be found much moral energy and a great deal of social activity which accounted for a very significant amount of political and economic activity.

An even clearer explanation of Calvin's thought proved that Christian liberty found little room for growth:

[37] Ibid., 128–129.

> The Genevan thinker was a logician rather than a philosopher, a rigorous system maker and dogmatist who knotted every argument and tied every strand securely into its fellow, till there was no escape from the net unless one broke through the mesh. To the formalist who demanded an exact system, and to the timid who feared free speculation, the logical consistency of Calvinism made irresistible appeal; and this perhaps suffices to explain its extraordinary hold on the rank and file of middle-class English Presbyterians.[38]

Throughout that portion of Europe which had become protestantized, centuries of medieval art had been destroyed, and the entire Catholic liturgical calendar—with its annual cycle of feasts, fasts, and the entirety of its religious drama—was no more. Any Marian theology, let alone public displays of devotion to the Blessed Virgin, were passé, as were pilgrimages to her shrines, or the shrines of any of the saints of centuries past, and so on. The result? A sort of worldly asceticism replaced the contemplative spirit Catholicism had assumed for centuries:

> The absence of natural theology and liturgical comforts left the lonely soul face to face with the transcendent (and therefore elusive) will of God. This will had to be sought and served not through our contemplations but directly through our practice. From the solitude and uncertainty of that position came the responsibility which could find no rest.[39]

[38] Vernon L. Parrington, *Main Currents in American Thought: The Colonial Mind, 1620–1800, Volume 1* (New York: Harcourt Brace and Company, 1954), 12.

[39] Grant, 23.

In the practical realm, the American colonies saw various forms of Protestantism, ranging from the established Anglican Church, to the various forms of Calvinistic, Puritan expression, to followers of Luther, to the most peaceable and religiously tolerant Quakers. The more staunch among adherents in these various sects might well oppose the presence of others, but "the full force of Puritan vigor was directed against those who professed 'popery' ... it was immaterial that Puritans, when persecuted in Virginia, had found welcome and asylum in Maryland."[40] It had not been the Puritan intention (or, for that matter, any other religious sect) to secularize culture. Puritans especially wanted to raise the standard of religious knowledge and practice; the sermon was to replace the liturgy, Bible reading would quickly supersede religious imagery and symbols; pilgrimages, so frequent in the medieval world, were now replaced by a sort of piety which rested in the individual himself. The commercial and industrial classes in England and Holland were equally attracted to this, especially to a downplaying of any type of external display—rather, industry and frugality were seen as paramount.

Such attitudes were to be found in colonial Maryland as much as the other colonies, and it was this sort of mentality which prevailed at the time of Charles Carroll the Settler's arrival in the colony until his death in 1720. It is true that each generation of the Carroll family was usually viewed, because of their enormous wealth, as constituting a separate entity beyond many of the prescriptions against their coreligionists. This may also have contributed to their ability to remain constantly steadfast in their religious beliefs and practices.

[40] Charles H. Metzger, S.J., *Catholics and the American Revolution* (Chicago: Loyola University Press, 1962), 5.

We are able to catch only glimpses of the closeness the Settler had to his Catholic Faith. He did send his three boys—Henry, Daniel, and Charles—to study at the college of the English Jesuits in St. Omer, French Flanders, and of those three, Henry would lose his life at an early age, en route back from his studies. The Settler conveyed the news to his two remaining sons:

> I suppose you have before this time, had the afflicting news of your brother's death within about six days saile of the Capes of Virginia as he was coming in; it was upon the 10th day of April last. I hope you both know your duty upon so lamentable an occasion. The most that you and I or any other of his relations and friends can doe for him now is to pray for the repose of his soul, wherein I desire you will not be deficient, nor in minding the sodality whereof he was a member, of what is usual to be done on such occasions.[41]

The Settler died just one year after writing this letter. His son Charles would become known as Charles Carroll of Annapolis, and his son Daniel, the youngest of the five children who lived, would marry Ann Rozier, daughter of Notley Rozier of Notley Hall, Maryland, and began the Carrolls of Duddington, Prince George's County. Duddington estate encompassed the land on which the United States Capitol now stands.[42]

41 Charles Carroll the Settler to Charles and Daniel Carroll, July 7, 1719, cited in Rowland, 10. "What is usual to be done" is almost certainly a reference to having Masses offered for the repose of his soul.

42 In the rectory of St. Peter's Church on Capitol Hill are to be found pieces of religious artwork and a fireplace, all originally a part of Duddington.

Upon the Settler's death, the Lieutenant Governor, Sharpe, wrote to the current Lord Baltimore of his day informing him that "one Mr. Carroll, a Roman Catholic, died here and left a considerable estate to his two sons, having appointed two of his relatives their guardians and executors of his last will and testament."[43] The Settler obviously bequeathed the same sort of militant Catholicism to his sons, and, for his part, Charles Carroll of Annapolis (who had been born in 1702) had a religious faith which:

> reflected the influence of the Jesuits who had shaped him. He did not question the teachings of the Church; he was (as his son would become) a devout Roman Catholic, who believed that strict doctrinal adherence was essential for salvation ... When his father died, he engaged priests to say Mass for him. He married Elizabeth Brooke in a ceremony that complied precisely with the format prescribed by the Council of Trent, and upon her death he had Masses offered for her in Maryland, and forwarded (his son) money for similar services in England. He prayed regularly, and maintained a "Priest's Room" at Doughoregan. He wanted a priest nearby to say Mass, to help him make his Easter duty, which included Confession, to give him the Last Rights, to absolve him from sin.[44]

[43] Those referred to are his two brothers-in-law and his kinsmen James and Daniel Carroll. Sharpe noted that when the will was first probated, the kinsmen were of the same religion as the testator, though one of them eventually gave up the Faith and was publicly denounced by the other. The matter was taken up by the Colonial Assembly which resolved that "Papists were bad members of the community." Rowland, 13.

[44] Hoffman and Mason, 280. See also Connor, 145.

The Settler's death in 1720 dashed all hopes for his son to pursue legal studies at the conclusion of his coursework at Douai. He left his brother Daniel to complete his studies, sailed for home, took up residence at his mother's home in Annapolis, and placed himself under the tutelage of a cousin, James Carroll, the active trustee of the Settler's estate. This is not to suggest he considered his time in France to be in any way wasted; in fact, his respect for the Jesuits who taught him only increased. They seemed to personify qualities he deemed essential—"austerity, steadfastness, integrity, and discipline combined with the reasoned use of the mind." He especially honored them because "they refused to compromise their adherence to ecclesiastical doctrine and never wavered in their central mission: protecting the true church from heresy through faith and reason and restoring it to absolute dominance."[45]

No sooner back in his native Maryland, Charles of Annapolis lost no time in setting into action a course of events which allowed him to build on the huge fortune the Settler had amassed and continue in the same stead.

> Denied access to political power, Charles Carroll of Annapolis turned his considerable energies to attaining wealth as the only available means of securing the Carroll foothold in Maryland. With considerable acumen, he set about reassembling the Settler's estate which had been parceled out to his mother, his sisters, and brother, since by consolidating their portions he controlled considerably more working capital than that which would have been available to him from his share alone ... by 1731 ... in partnership with Benjamin Tasker, Daniel Dulany, and a Protestant cousin, Dr. Charles Carroll,

[45] Ibid.

> [he] was able to invest 3,500 [pounds] in establishing the Baltimore Iron Works on the banks of the Patapsco River. By 1764 this venture was yielding him about 400 [pounds] annually. In addition, he continued to expand his father's money—lending operations and estimated by the mid-1760s that he had in excess of 24,000 [pounds] at interest.[46]

Charles of Annapolis's "extraordinary drive to enlarge his fortune was matched by his determination to fashion an heir mentally and morally fit to receive and preserve that grand legacy,"[47] and this became a reality in Annapolis on September 8, 1737, when Charles of Annapolis and his "wife" Elizabeth Brooke welcomed into the world their only child, Charles Carroll of Carrollton, future signer of the Declaration of Independence, and affectionately called "Charley." Older historians would write about it in this vein:

> Charles Carroll of Annapolis married Elizabeth Brooke, daughter of Clement Brooke and Jane Sewell. The wife was well connected and was distantly related to her husband in two or three ways. Her people were Catholic landholders, educated and wealthy. One son was born and was named Charles, who became Charles Carroll of Carrollton, one of the very influential and conspicuous figures in colonial and national politics. The father lived to see his son achieve great honor as a statesman, but the mother died when he was only twenty-four years old.[48]

46 Ann C. Van Devanter, "*Anywhere So Long As There Be Freedom*": *Charles Carroll of Carrollton, His Family & His Maryland* (Baltimore: The Baltimore Museum of Art, 1975), "Charles Carroll of Carrollton and His Family, 1688–1832," 16.

47 Ibid.

48 Lewis A. Leonard, *Life of Charles Carroll of Carrollton* (New York: Moffat, Yard and Company, 1918), 51.

Such formal pronouncements were common in an era not given to the "reality" to be found in more contemporary accounts. In fact, it is claimed that the Signer's parents lived in a common law marriage for twenty years and were joined sacramentally in matrimony only in 1757. Many theories have been advanced about it, the earliest being that Elizabeth Brooke was of a more socially inferior background than Charles of Annapolis. Such is given little credence today; it is true she did not come from anywhere near the financial status of the Carrolls, and she worked as a servant in Doughoregan Manor. At the same time, her mother's family were solidly Catholic—her maternal grandfather, Major Nicholas Sewall of Mattapany, St. Mary's County in Southern Maryland, was the stepson of Charles Calvert, third Lord Baltimore, and had fought valiantly for him in Coode's Rebellion, one of the major events in Maryland Colonial history which sought to overthrow proprietary (and therefore Catholic) interests. Her paternal grandfather, Major Thomas Brooke of Calvert County, had been raised a Protestant, converted to Catholicism at the time of his marriage, and raised his family solidly in the Faith. His eldest son reverted to Anglicanism, but three other sons became Jesuit priests. Further, from all accounts, Elizabeth Carroll fit well into the social structure of her environs and was well received by Chesapeake society. It would then appear that economic reasons proved a major component in their decision.

> The protection of the Carroll family fortune seems plausible. By keeping their marriage one of common law, Charles of Annapolis would be protected from the dower right—a legalism which entitled a widow to one-third of her late husband's fortune, as well as a

> guardianship right, yet another legalism which allowed her to control the other two-thirds in the name of any of her children not yet of legal age. In this case, a widow like Elizabeth Carroll would have access to such a tremendous fortune, she would easily have been prey to a gold digger who would have moved the Carroll legacy in a very different direction, more than likely into a Protestant family circumstance. If, however, Charles of Annapolis remained unmarried, or died leaving no offspring, the Carroll family would have retained control, and such fortune, according to a will he drew up about 1760, would have passed to his relative, Daniel Carroll of Rock Creek.[49]

The spiritual and ecclesial dimensions are of even greater importance. In Church history, her laws regarding marriage, especially in Protestant countries, were intricate and complex. Marriage is one of the Church's seven sacraments, just as divinely instituted as the other six, but a sacrament which is conferred on the partners by each other, with the priest as merely the Church's official witness. Until the middle of the sixteenth century, the Church recognized the validity of mutual agreement without the presence of an ordained priest. These unions were called "clandestine marriages," and the Church considered the partners committed to each other for life, their children were considered legitimate, and any attempt to extricate oneself from the union for another partner was looked on as bigamy. As the years went on, the Church began to express her preference for solemnizing a marriage in the presence of a priest but did not invalidate

[49] Van Devanter, 17–18. Daniel Carroll of Rock Creek was one of two Catholic signers of the U.S. Constitution, and brother of Archbishop John Carroll, the country's first bishop.

those that were not. It was not until the Council of Trent (1545–1563) that the decree *Tametsi* was promulgated, though such decree could not take effect until it was publicly proclaimed within a "formal ecclesiastical establishment." This was no difficulty in Catholic countries where civil authorities easily gave consent, but in places like England and her North American colonies where no formal Catholic organization existed, such proclamation was impossible; marriages of Catholics in colonial Maryland had to continue in the same fashion—the mutual consent of the parties. The Carrolls' marriage could have fallen within the understanding of pre-Tridentine times, and it is unlikely a sacramental marriage prior to 1757 could have taken place, since the officiant, knowing such, would never have signed the sacramental register, which reads:

> I Mathias Manners a Priest of the Society of Jesus do hereby certify that I did on the 15th day of February in the year of Our Lord 1757 marry Charles Carroll Esq: and Elizabeth Brooke daughter of Clement Brooke Esq. late of Prince George's County deceased.
>
> In testimony whereof I have hereunto set my hand, and affixed my Seal the day and year first above mentioned
>
> testeth
> Jane Brooke   Mathias Manners, S.J.
> John Ireland[50]

Yet another historical account points out that Maryland Catholics were still under penal law, and the record of a sacramental marriage witnessed by a priest would have been invalidated by Maryland civil law:

[50] Hoffman and Mason, 136–138.

> Nor does this certificate of itself establish that Carroll's parents did not enjoy a sacramental marriage in the eyes of the Catholic Church, making him a legitimate child regardless of what civil law said. The presence and witness of a priest was not required for sacramental validity in the Maryland region at this time. The consent of the couple was the essential element; the right might be supplied later for a number of good reasons. In fact the promulgation of this requirement of a priest lagged even in Catholic countries; and about four years after the marriage of Carroll's parents was initiated the pope was urging promulgation in these countries. Unless promulgated, the priestly rite was not necessary for sacramental validity ... The good standing of Carroll's parents with the Church and its clergy should be noted in records of this time. This could hardly have been possible if they did not enjoy a sacramental marriage and were in the eyes of the Catholic community living in sinful concubinage, for which they should be avoided lest further scandal be given.[51]

Evidence for Charles Carroll's initial illegitimacy was further proven some sixty years after his death by the testimony of one Anna Hanson McKinney Dorsey, a noted nineteenth-century author who contributed to, among other publications, *Ave Maria Magazine*, long published by the Holy Cross Fathers at the University of Notre Dame in South Bend, Indiana.[52] In correspondence with Fr. Daniel

[51] Thomas O'Brien Hanley, S.J., *Charles Carroll of Carrollton: The Making of a Revolutionary Gentleman* (Chicago: Loyola University Press, 1982), 267.

[52] Mrs. Dorsey, a friend of Charles Carroll's granddaughters, was a native of Washington, DC, who had converted to Catholicism in 1840. In 1889, the Centenary Year of the establishment

Hudson, C.S.C., longtime editor of the publication, she shared with him information she had gotten through the years:

> As Charles the future Signer was completing his course of studies at St. Omer's in French Flanders, his father wrote him to enjoy a brief sojourn in Europe, and then return home. The younger Carroll, who did not heed his father's advice, replied that he would never return until his father had married his mother. The next letter he received from Charles of Annapolis sent word of his parents' sacramental marriage.

In a further missive to Hudson, Mrs. Dorsey said the marital arrangement was well known in Maryland, and the eventual marriage was viewed by most as adding to the glory, rather than the shame of an already noble life. Further, Mrs. Dorsey had had a conversation with a Fr. Griffin, a longtime friend and a priest who had served for many years as chaplain to the Carrolls at Doughoregan Manor, and asked him if it were true. "It is true," he replied, "but people revere the memory of the old signer so deeply, and have such respect for his family, that no one ever speaks of it, in fact it is unknown to the present generation."[53]

It is a curious turn of events how Charles of Annapolis could have lived comfortably with his arrangement, given

---

of the American Hierarchy, James Cardinal Gibbons of Baltimore presented her with Notre Dame's Laetare Medal, the Church's highest lay award, for her contribution to the development of American Catholic literature.

[53] Anna Hanson McKenney Dorsey to Fr. Daniel Hudson, C.S.C., Feb. 27, 1892; July 21, 1892. Both cited in Hoffman and Mason, 399–400. Hudson was editor of *Ave Maria Magazine*, published at Norte Dame.

his fierce attachment to his Catholic Faith. One of his biographers has posited that "discipline and reason, not sentiment and sensibility, marked his behavior and attachments." His pride in his Irish heritage, for example, "did not include a romantic longing for the country of his fathers," while he "saw no contradiction between religious belief and an examination of Enlightenments ideals. Hence, Voltaire could sit beside his missal." Even more to the point, "he prized independence of mind and did not regard rational inquiry and religious faith as mutually contradictory."[54] Mere snippets into his mindset, to be sure, but perhaps offering a clue.

Regardless of their situation, Charles of Annapolis and Elizabeth Brooke welcomed their son into the world on September 19, 1737, in Annapolis. His youthful years have been described as "happy and uneventful,"[55] though for sure they were spent in far more elegant surroundings than the majority of colonials experienced. The home in which he was born is still to be seen in Annapolis, facing Spa Creek, on the grounds of what is today Old St. Mary's parish, under the direction of the Redemptorist Fathers.[56] One view of the birthplace described it as a "large and commodious brick dwelling house ... containing eleven fine rooms without—houses, gardens, and stables. It is beautifully situated on an eminence commanding a delightful prospect of the bay and surrounding country and for

[54] Ibid., 279, 281.

[55] Smith, 27. Prior to his beginning formal education, Carroll's major biographers offer little in the way of particulars of his earliest years.

[56] The house was given to the Redemptorists in 1852 by Carroll's daughter, Mary Carroll Caton.

those fond of pleasure there is fine fishing and ducking in the vicinity."[57]

It is somewhat difficult for the modern mind to appreciate the tremendous difficulties under which Catholics in both England and the American colonies had to operate. The Maryland Colony was just slightly more than a century old when Charles Carroll of Carrollton, or Charley as he immediately became known, was born. In that period of time, scores of pieces on anti-Catholic legislation had been passed in his native colony as well as all the others. The courage these people showed has been well captured:

> As the cleavage with the Catholic past widened in England, the education of Catholic boys and girls became more and more difficult, and an outlaw race of schools, colleges, and seminaries was begun "beyond the seas." The schools in the English colonies were regulated by the same penal code as prevailed in England, and Catholic children could enter only at the price of their Faith. It was against the law to employ a Catholic tutor, though as the years went by the law fell into abeyance, especially towards the end of the eighteenth century. It was equally unlawful, in fact treasonable, for Catholics to send their children to the English Catholic colleges on the Continent; but as is well known, Catholic parents felt no hesitation in allowing their boys and girls, despite their tender years, to run the risk of capture, in order that they might receive a Catholic education.[58]

[57] *Baltimore American and Daily Commercial Advertiser*. March 25, 1844. Cited in Van Devanter, 73. Mary Caton had likely been trying to sell the house at first; when attempts did not succeed, the decision was made to give it to the religious congregation.

[58] Peter Guilday, *The Life and Times of John Carroll, Archbishop of Baltimore: 1715–1735* (New York: The Encyclopedia Press, 1922),

The Carroll family has been well described here, and considering their affluence and their social standing in Maryland colonial life (despite their religious faith), it would be expected that a young man like Charley would receive the finest of Catholic education. In fact, Charles of Annapolis's "extraordinary drive to enlarge his fortune was matched by his determination to fashion an heir mentally and morally fit to receive and preserve that grand legacy."[59] As such, the Jesuits were to play as substantial a role in Charley's education as they had in his father's and grandfather's. That influence was not found solely on the Continent, however—it would have its beginnings in his native colony.

---

cited in Joseph Gurn, *Charles Carroll of Carrollton: 1737–1832* (New York: P.J. Kenedy & Sons, 1932), 7.

59 Van Devanter, 16.

CHAPTER 2

THE FORMATIVE YEARS

It is a curious and providential part of Maryland colonial history, that despite ongoing periods of intense anti-Catholic discrimination, especially in the education of Catholic children, schools nonetheless rose up and had quite successful histories of bequeathing to those same children their Catholic heritage, doctrine, and the rudiments of fine education. One such attempt was on Maryland's eastern shore, near the present-day town of Warwick. Among the reasons for this particular spiritual outreach was its proximity to the religiously tolerant colony of Pennsylvania, founded by William Penn and his Quaker settlers, well known for their broadmindedness to all Christian sects in the practice of their respective creeds. English Jesuit Fr. Thomas Mansell had ministered for some years to the Catholic settlers in this area of Cecil County, and a grant of land situated on Little Bohemia Creek had been surveyed as early as 1683 for two sisters, Marian and Margaret O'Daniell. They in turn promised the land to Fr. Mansell and a layman, William Douglass. The Jesuit later purchased Douglass's portion, and upon the tract of 458 acres, built Saint Xaverius

Mission, named for St. Francis Xavier, the famed Jesuit missionary to India and Japan.

Forty-one years later, another English Jesuit, Fr. Thomas Poulton, opened an academy for boys, grade-school age, by contemporary standards. There is little known about the school because "the Jesuit Fathers were too wise to set down records which, if found, would circumstantially sentence them to life imprisonment."[60] Subsequent historical investigations have uncovered, however, the names of scores of boys who attended the school. One scholar has at least ventured that Old Bohemia Academy sought to lay the foundation of a "practical and useful education," by emphasizing areas to which little attention was given in the schools of the day: "bookkeeping, the rudiments of surveying and navigation, as well as the classics."[61] In addition to the original mission, there is concrete evidence that a separate building was constructed to house the academy, and it was around that building—which served as both school and residence for the boys who came from all parts of the Maryland Colony and elsewhere—that the life of the mission plantation centered.

It is known that among the Academy's earliest students were Daniel Carroll, eleven, of Rock Creek, who would go on to be one of two Catholic signers of the U.S. Constitution, as well as his brother John Carroll, the country's first Catholic bishop. Older accounts of Charles Carroll matter-of-factly had him among this early group as well, but the mission's most authoritative accounts note that although there is a persistent tradition to this effect, there is "no

[60] Smith, 29.
[61] Leonard, 51.

documentary evidence to prove that Charles Carroll of Carrollton also attended Bohemia Academy before studying in Europe."[62]

Bohemia seems to have opened and closed spasmodically, and its activity was regulated by the Colonial Assembly as the temper of the time dictated. As long as colonial attention was fixed on other matters than restricting Catholics, all was fine and education for the many boys in attendance went on as normal. When, however, the political climate altered, in periods of "true official zeal" as they have been called, "the school was closed completely, the boys sent home, and nobody knew a thing in the world about it."[63]

What is known with a high degree of accuracy is the course of higher education pursued by so many of Maryland's Catholic young men, especially those of substantial means. Catholic colleges on the Continent were well known in colonial America, and seen as a threat by many in the Protestant political ascendancy:

> The effect of ... continental education on young Catholic gentlemen was clearly seen. As a class they were far superior to their Protestant neighbors, who, educated at home, were narrow and insular in their ideas, ignorant of modern languages and of all that was going on beyond their country limits and its fox hunts and races. The Catholic, on the contrary, was conversant with several languages, with the current literature of Europe, the science of the day, with art and the great galleries

[62] Rev. Thomas J. Peterman, *Bohemia: 1704–2004: A History of Saint Francis Xavier Catholic Shrine in Cecil County, Maryland* (Devon, Pennsylvania: William T. Cooke Publishing, Inc., 2004), 34.

[63] Smith, 29.

> where the masterpieces of painting and sculpture could be seen. He returned to England or his colonial home after forming acquaintance with persons of distinction and influence, whose correspondence retained and enlarged the knowledge he had acquired.[64]

Of all the continental English Catholic schools, St. Omer's in French Flanders was "best loved by the boys of Maryland."[65] The school's origin can be traced to 1566, when Gerard d'Hamericourt, Bishop of St. Omer, invited the Society of Jesus to set up a college there. It quickly acquired the reputation of the finest school in the French Netherlands, and the growth of the student body, along with the admiration of the Catholic faithful who sent their sons there, hastened the decision of the English Jesuits to come there to establish their own institution in 1593. The founder of the English school was Fr. Robert Persons, already a well-established figure in the Society. Born in Somerset to yeoman parents, he was ordained in Rome in 1575 and accompanied St. Edmund Campion on his clandestine mission to persecuted English Catholics in 1580. After the latter's capture, incarceration in the Tower of London, and eventual martyrdom, the English Jesuit provincial deemed it unwise for the Jesuits to endanger themselves further in an atmosphere of such anti-Catholic hostility. When Persons left England, he was never to return; he went first to Spain, where, successful with a number of conciliatory efforts to win the favor of King Philip II, he

[64] *Catholic Record Society*, "Memoir of Edmund Mathew," ii, 29, cited in Guilday, 22.

[65] Peter Guilday, *The Life and Times of John Carroll, Archbishop of Baltimore* (New York: The Encyclopedia Press, 1922), 17. Among the others, the best remembered were at Douai in France (later reestablished at Rheims) and Valladolid in Spain.

made use of the royal favor he had won to establish the English colleges at Valladolid, Seville, Madrid, and Lisbon, before beginning his efforts at St. Omer.[66] It was apparently his like for the weather of his native land that made him choose St. Omer, "for no part thereof liked him better than the Low Countries in regard to their nearness to England and air most like unto the air of our English climate."[67] St. Henry Walpole had been serving as bursar at Valladolid but longed to return to England for missionary work; through his friendship with Philip II, he was able to secure a royal charter for the new school at St. Omer and promised to send funds. In his plan, Fr. Persons expected the college at Douai to send recruits to Rome for the English College (Seminary) which Cardinal William Allen was instrumental in establishing, while his own school at St. Omer would provide men for the Spanish seminaries.[68] As to the new school itself:

> The Constitutions for St. Omers College followed closely those prepared for Valladolid. They differed in this, that boys who went to St. Omers made no promise to become priests. If they decided to go forward to the priesthood, these went from St. Omers to Valladolid. Boys were admitted to the college at fourteen. They had

66 St. Omer is considered the forerunner of Stonyhurst College, in "old Catholic Lancashire," near the present-day city of Preston in northern England. In 1596, Seville, Persons wrote his famous *Memorial for the Reformation of England,* which provided a type of blueprint for the envisioned society England was to become after its return to the true Faith.

67 Hubert Chadwick, *St. Omers to Stonyhurst* (London: Burns and Oates, 1962), "Historical Memorials for the Rector of St. Omer's," 12.

68 Because of the times, St. Omer was given the code name, or alias, *Flamstead* among the Jesuits.

> to be English or from greater Britain; if living in exile, both their parents had to be English and Catholic. A knowledge of Latin was obligatory and, outside the times of recreation, Latin was spoken throughout the school.[69]

Above all, the College of St. Omer, known for its strict allegiance to the Catholic Faith, was a true beacon of light for English Catholics and served as one of the strongest witnesses to truth in Counter Reformation times. A closer look at the curriculum tells a particular story:

> The Arts (drama, dance, music and poetry) occupied an important place in the curriculum. Pupils also learned such values as living in a community, sociability and solidarity. These principles of education, working against the backdrop of the Enlightenment in France, were a strong factor in the political choices and careers of American and British ex-pupils ... The rigorous education required a mastery of Latin and Greek and sought to transmit the moral values of the Jesuit *Ratio Studiorum*. The school grew rapidly and counted around 200 pupils in the first two decades of the 17th century, further contributing to the reputation of excellence of the teaching given in Saint-Omer. It spread as far as the Catholic communities of the new American state, reaching the Carroll, Neale or Calvert families for example.[70]

The college quickly became well known in the colonies, and the Assemblies of Virginia and Maryland "both sent petitions at odd times to the Home Government, representing

[69] Bernard Basset, S.J., *The English Jesuits: From Campion to Martindale* (New York: Herder & Herder, 1968), 80.

[70] *LA FAMILLE CARROLL: Itinéraire du Maryland à Saint-Omer* (Saint-Omer: Saint-Omer Flandre Intérieure, 2017), 20, 53.

the danger which St. Omer's was to the Protestant ascendancy in the provinces."[71] By his own admission, Charles Carroll spent five and one-half years there before going on to Rheims to begin further advanced studies.[72]

His years at St. Omer, begun as a boy of only eleven years,[73] was an experience which he seems to have greatly appreciated from the beginning. Writing to his father at the age of thirteen, he realized the degree of paternal care which made Charles of Annapolis choose his alma mater for his son:

> I can easily see the great affection you have for Me by sending me hear [*sic*] to a Colege [*sic*] where I may not only be a learned man, but also be advanced in piety and devotion.[74]

Charley (as his family always called him) reciprocated the great favor his father had accorded him by sending him abroad for his education. By the time of his leave-taking in November 1753, the headmaster Fr. John Jenison described him as "the finest young man, in every respect, that ever

[71] Guilday, 21.

[72] Charles Carroll of Carrollton to the Countess of Auzouer, September 20, 1771: *Maryland Historical Magazine*, xxxii, 207, cited in Smith, 34. Some of the other dates Carroll included in this letter detailing his entire sojourn in Europe have been questioned by some historians for accuracy.

[73] This is three years younger than the age cited by Basset; there may well have been an exception made because of the wealth and influence of the Carroll family, or, noted by the same author, was the addition of a preparatory school at Boulogne-sur-Mer, though none of Carroll's biographers make mention of his attending it.

[74] Charles Carroll of Carrollton to Charles Carroll of Annapolis, March 1751, cited in Bradley J. Birzer, *American Cicero: The Life of Charles Carroll* (Wilmington, Delaware: ISI Books, 2010), 4.

enter'd the house," one whose "sweet temper rendered him equally agreeable both to equals and superiors," and most importantly, "a young man whose application to his Book and Devotions was constant and unchangeable."[75] Of each of the schools Charley attended in Europe, St. Omer seems to have left the most lasting impression on him. Decades later, as an old man, he confided his memories to his close friend Fr. Charles Constantine Pise, a Baltimore priest and one-time chaplain of the U.S. Congress. Fr. Pise recalled of Carroll that often:

> In the retirement of his old age, in the social hours of his evening fireside, have I heard him speak in strains of the highest eulogy, and with sentiments of the most devoted attachment, and expressions of the noblest gratitude, of his ancient preceptors. To them he attributed all that he knew—to their solicitude he referred all that he valued in his acquirements; and particularly that deep and hallowed conviction of religious truth, which was the ornament of his youth, and the solace of his old age. When anyone uttered a sentiment of astonishment how, in his advanced years, he could rise so early, and kneel so long—these good practices he would answer with his high tone of cheerfulness, I learned under the Jesuits, at the College of St. Omers [*sic*].[76]

If nothing else, St. Omer had instilled a life of discipline in the young Carroll. Each day began with Mass at 5:00 a.m., followed by an intense schedule of study and classes. Fast friendships were formed, especially with young English Catholic gentlemen,

[75] John Jenison to Charles Carroll of Annapolis, November 1753, cited in ibid., 5.

[76] Ibid., 7–8.

in addition to fellow Catholic Marylanders. Spiritual formation had been equally rich; Fr. Levinus Browne, S.J., held the title Director of Spiritual Life and was himself a recognized authority in his field, as well as having held significant positions in the English Jesuit Province. Browne had a wonderful ability to teach the *Spiritual Exercises of St. Ignatius* to both laymen and students. Days of retreat based on these *Exercises* were held annually at the school, attendance mandatory, along with a thorough grounding in catechism—more than likely, the *Catechism of the Council of Trent*. Also, the works of Fr. Robert Persons, S.J., one of the most recognizable of Jesuit names in this era, were studied in great detail; these included the *Directorium*, as well as the *Three Conversions of England*. Persons developed the idea of spiritual combat in one's personal life, but, given the period in which he was writing—the Protestant Reformation—he was one of the strongest of literary counter reformers. It was a time when the doctrines of the Faith must be upheld, understood, and more deeply appreciated —all elements Persons weaved into the fabric of his books. Finally, young men like Charley Carroll were introduced to the Sodality of the Blessed Virgin Mary, a strong Jesuit tradition which sought to inculcate personal piety based on Marian devotion with the active practice of the Christian virtues.

Once arrived at the Jesuit College at Rheims, a strong Jesuit spiritual foundation could only be built on all the more. Members of the Society had opened the College there in 1608, and it would be in operation until the suppression of the Jesuits in the eighteenth century. By the time of Charles Carroll's arrival, the college had declined somewhat in size, with 175 students, only fifty of whom were laymen. It boasted an impressive library of eighteen thousand books, as well as a series of theatres known to produce some of the finest theatrical performances of any of the Jesuit colleges on the Continent. History, geography, and even heraldry were studied in greater detail than at St. Omer, as was the study of poetic forms, which, by all accounts, young Carroll took little interest in. As the young man progressed in his studies and personal maturity, these years appear to have been a time when his father, Charles of Annapolis, began taking an even greater interest in his son's development, and in the amount of fatherly advice he began to offer. By fall of 1755, he was ready, academically and temperamentally, to proceed to Paris for his philosophical studies. These were taken at the *Lycée Louis-le-Grand*, which had been begun by the Jesuits in 1563 as the *College de Clermont* but renamed for Louis XIV in the 1680s when the monarch was at the apex of his career. Situated in Paris's famed Latin Quarter, a part of the city which had been home to students for centuries, it was in close proximity to the Sorbonne and other historic French universities. It was geared to educate the French elite, and many of its graduates became influential statesmen, diplomats, writers, artists, intellectuals, scientists, and members of the French Catholic hierarchy. Charles Carroll was to reside at *L'Hôtel de Saint-Louis Rue,* in the district of Saint-Antoine, where many English students were to be found. As in the past, Jesuit education and spirituality were found in the person of Fr. Edward Galloway, master and tutor at the residence—an English Jesuit more than familiar with the conditions (and hardships) facing coreligionists in England, knowledge which would be beneficial to young Carroll as he journeyed further in his European education.

His Parisian experience has been succinctly captured:

> The fullness of cultural life was found in Paris in the eighteenth century, but here was also an aura of civic majesty, which provoked reflection as well as mood. The College of Louis the Great was in the

midst of it all, and the Sun King made it his favorite benefaction. The Jesuit theological and cultural tradition was hostile to the Jansenist message of this era which originated in its most eloquent seventeenth century spokesman, Blaise Pascal. His *Provincial Letters* returned the volleys from Jesuit Colleges; Louis XIV shrewdly saw the Jesuits as a citadel against this theological enemy of the state, which prompted his patronage of the college named after him ... In philosophy, the college stood against the stream of Cartesianism, now considerably turned aside from the main current of French thought when Charles arrived at Paris. Finally, Protestantism had long been under counter-attack by Jesuit polemicists, and its French manifestation in the Huguenots literally drew the fire of Louis XIV's armies ... The new natural law trend, well under way in the eighteenth century with Locke and Montesquieu ... constituted a rich enlargement of the more traditional Aristotelian and Thomistic studies, and would be pursued by Charles at the college. There were many other subtle adjustments in the traditional Jesuit intellectual orientation. Just as the study of French gained emphasis in Charles' earlier years, so now the nationalism of eighteenth-century France called for patriotic themes in the Jesuit theatres at the college ... [Charles] had to learn the outlines of logic in the classic style which became the pattern of colonial and revolutionary rhetoric. Concurrently, this first year he strove to master the systematic metaphysics of Aristotle and Aquinas. Mathematics in the dress of Sir Isaac Newton was also studied and given further development with programs in physics his second year ... If his readings are any indication, this final year in which a comprehensive

> public defense of philosophy took place was also rich in seventeenth- and eighteenth-century thought, especially as it stemmed from John Locke.[77]

The Jesuit College at Brouges was an outgrowth of St. Omer; in 1762, due mostly to a rise in internal social tension, France expelled the Jesuits from the country. Priest faculty members and many students fled to the Austrian Netherlands, now a part of Belgium. The school would operate in Bruges Brouges for slightly more than a decade, after which it moved again to Liège.[78] The former locale saw Charles Carroll's matriculation to yet further studies, this time in French civil law. Here he delved deeply into philosophical reflections on the nature of civil law, aided by the writings of Montesquieu, especially *The Spirit of the Laws.* Natural law demanded specific governmental systems to

77 Hanley, 32–33. Jansenism was a theological movement prevalent especially in France, which emphasized Original Sin and its consequences, human depravity, the necessity of grace, and a strong emphasis on predestination. It found its way into seminaries, most notably in Ireland, and strongly affected the teaching of moral theology, giving it a rigorous interpretation. John Locke was a seventeenth-century political philosopher whose writings greatly influenced America's founding fathers, as well as the foundational documents of the United States.

78 In 1793, the French Revolution and England's declaration of war against France ended Jesuit educational efforts in France for a time. Remaining students returned to England, where a relaxation in the penal laws accorded Catholics greater freedom. An alumnus of the French years, Thomas Weld, donated a mansion and grounds for the English Jesuits to begin a college at Stonyhurst in Lancashire in the north of England. Coincidentally, Weld was a member of an old recusant Catholic family, longtime friends of the Carrolls of Maryland. It was in the chapel of Lulworth Castle, ancestral home of the Welds, that John Carroll was consecrated first Bishop of Baltimore.

avoid chaos and anarchy, and those who made and executed laws for the benefit of society exercised an authority in peoples' lives entirely different from judicial systems. At Brouges also, his studies allowed him to see Western Civilization as an "organic process of growth,"[79] which had as its basis an optimism stemming from the Enlightenment. A natural outgrowth of this was the view that civilization contained within it the law of progress, one which animated social reform in its varied expressions.

Voltaire also formed much of Charley's study at Brouges—a new set of ideas, to be sure. The young Marylander critically studied the Frenchman's critique of Christianity in such a way as not to be shaken by its implications. Indeed, Carroll's whole experience of English Catholicism in his native colony had been one of freedom—religious toleration to all forms of Christianity; he had known a Church neither "the Ultramontane nor the Gallican church of France,"[80] and hence could accept Voltaire's case for tolerance, despite his hostility to revealed religion. In spite of this, or perhaps because of it, Charles appears to have grown into a serious Christian gentleman:

> "I observe my religious duties . . . I trust in ye mercy of God not my own merits, which are none, & hope He will pardon my daily offenses . . . I retain as yet that salutary fear of His justice . . . which by ye wisest of men is stiled *initium sapientiae* . . . I love Him[,]tho 'far

79 Hanley, 63.

80 Ibid., 64. *Ultramontane* is a term usually referring to the concept of "more Roman than Rome," not allowing for any worldly contamination, whereas *Gallican* would infer a co-existence, if not a subservience to the state.

> less than His infinite goodness deserves & I would wish to do."[81]

Charley was not especially taken with Brouges and decided to return to his former college in Paris to complete his studies in French law. Within the walls of the *College Louis-le-Grand*, he "recaptured the excitement of three years before."[82] From there, he would continue on to London, where he arrived in September 1759, for a yet deeper immersion in the study of English law. As with all his previous studies, Charley was enrolled in the finest judicial educational experience the mother country had to offer—the Inner Temple:

> The word "Inn" has always had a special meaning of mansion or town house and, in particular, one used as a hostel for barristers and students ... The Inns date ... probably from the fourteenth century, and it is believed they came into existence for the purpose of teaching, controlling and protecting bodies of "apprentices", i.e. students and barristers below the rank of Serjeant-At-Law ... The need for proper instruction in the English Common Law (not taught in the universities) led to the establishment in the early thirteenth century of hostels for practitioners and students within easy reach of Westminster ... Legal education at the Inns of Court originally extended over a period of seven or eight years and consisted of lectures given by senior barristers (Readers) followed by discussions ... In addition, history, music and dancing were taught

81 Charles Carroll of Carrollton to Charles Carroll of Annapolis, January 17, 1759, cited in ibid., 65.

82 Ibid., 68.

> with a view to preparing the students to play their part suitably in the higher levels of society.[83]

His London years would constitute the last part of his sojourn in Europe—one which lasted seventeen years. During this time, much had occurred in his native land, and the older and more mature Charley became, the more frequently his father kept him abreast of events. Such missives began during the French and Indian War, or, as it was known in Europe, the Seven Years' War, which came to its final conclusion with the signing of the peace treaty at Ghent, Belgium, in 1763.

> [The] French and Indian War ... was the final struggle between the French government, and its colonies in America, and the English government and its colonies in America for imperialistic control of the North American Continent. In its broader aspect, it was the result of the clash between French and English colonial frontiers. As such, it was a part of and was overshadowed by the Seven Years' War which embroiled Europe from 1756 to 1763. In its narrower aspect, however, it was the result of the rivalry of French and English colonists in North America.[84]

English settlements were found along the eastern seaboard from Maine to Florida and to the west as far as the Appalachian Mountains; French settlements, by contrast, developed from fur trading posts found from the mouth of

83 Ben Weinreb and Christopher Hibbert, *The London Encyclopedia* (London: MacMillan Publishers, Ltd., 1987), 409–410. This account claims the Inner Temple, the school Charles Carroll attended, begun in 1505.

84 Wayne Andrews, *Concise Dictionary of American History* (New York: Charles Scribner's Sons, 1962), 383.

the St. Lawrence River to the Great Lakes; along the Great Lakes and in a southward direction along the Mississippi River to St. Louis and New Orleans. Both the French and the English vied for control of the fur trade, while a further rivalry existed between both nations along the eastern seaboard for fishing privileges off the coast of Newfoundland in Canada. The outbreak of the war had placed Catholics in a difficult position; rumors flew about a conspiracy in Maryland between Catholics and indigenous Indian tribes to overthrow British rule. A minister, Rev. Thomas Chase,[85] preached from his pulpit that Catholics were preparing to massacre Protestants; a Catholic priest, it was rumored, had been seen in the garb of a French officer; Black slaves were also poised to join the insurrection. One James Sterling, a Protestant Divine implored all "sons of the Reformation [to] guard your holy religion from Papal persecution, idolatry, gunpowder treasons, and worse than Smithfield fires!"[86] This sort of hysteria provoked the Maryland Colonial Assembly to impose stricter laws against Catholics; priests would have to "register their names and post bond for their good behavior,"[87] while those caught in the act of instructing converts to the Faith would be accused of (and usually convicted of) treason. Anyone educated at one of the Catholic institutions on the Continent could not own property, nor inherit the same.

[85] The father of Samuel Chase who, along with Charles Carroll of Carrollton, was a signer of the Declaration of Independence.

[86] McDermott, 44. The reference to Smithfield Fires was an event occurring near the end of the reign of Queen Mary Tudor in England, in the mid-sixteenth century, in which were martyred such Protestant leaders as Thomas Cranmer, Nicholas Ridley, Hugh Lattimer, John Hooper, et al.

[87] Ibid.

Even with such restrictions, Catholic Marylanders strongly favored the British cause during the war—Charles of Annapolis hoped for a time when "all French America will be our own,"[88] while his son Charley praised "our late glorious success at sea."[89] Despite this, Catholics in Maryland were barred from militia duty, and a double tax was imposed on all the lands they owned. Carroll of Annapolis along with fellow disgruntled coreligionists sent a sharp letter to the Governor, as might be expected, to no ultimate avail.

No sooner had Charley arrived in London than he sent off a letter to his father, in light of current anti-popery outbursts, expressing shock at how arbitrary such anti-Catholic legislation was, and how it occurred in the aftermath of whatever propagandizing happened to be uppermost at the given moment. He could not conceive "how any Roman Catholick [*sic*] especially an Irish Roman Catholick [*sic*] can consent to Live in England or any [of] the British dominions, if he is able to do otherwise." He also admitted that, "It's true we are quiet and unmolested at present, because the reigning king is not prejudiced against us; but the most tyrannical [*sic*] laws are still subsisting, they can be put into execution to day to morrow, whenever it shall please the King for the Parliament wou'd always [*sic*] readily comply with such a demand."[90] Such thoughts were anything but new to Charley or his father. Despite their tremendous wealth, the Carrolls were in many ways as victimized by Maryland anti-Catholic legislation as

88 Charles Carroll of Annapolis to Charles Carroll of Carrollton, November 27, 1758, cited in ibid., 45.

89 Charles Carroll of Carrollton to Charles Carroll of Annapolis, May 16, 1760, cited in ibid.

90 Charles Carroll of Carrollton to Charles Carroll of Annapolis, December 10, 1759, cited in Birzer, 20.

any of their coreligionists. As early as 1750, Charles of Annapolis had contrived a scheme for colonization by Maryland Catholics in territory which later became the state of Arkansas.

> Mr. Carroll selected a spot on the west side of the Arkansas river, commencing at its mouth and running a hundred and twenty miles up that river across to the Mississippi river, then to the place of beginning, at the mouth of the river Arkansas. Today this would be the splendid triangle with the Mississippi river as the western boundary and Little Rock and Memphis at the other two angles. This territory then belonged to the King of France with whose minister Mr. Carroll had conferred and was encouraged to believe the plan could be carried out.[91]

It was not, and a decade later Charles of Annapolis had reason for the regrets he surely entertained.

Charley seemed to be enjoying London to the full, though most of his biographers tend to agree that the study of English civil law to the depth he would be immersed in it did not strike a particularly resonant chord for his future life. First off, however, was his father's concern for his son's life in the English capital:

> If this meets you in London, it will meet you in an open and wide Ocean of danger: hitherto you have had friends to advise with, and good Example constantly before you; now you can only rely on God's grace, your own prudence and ye good principles instilled into you by a virtuous Education ... In your Situation ye greatest Resolution will be necessary to

[91] Leonard, 54.

> withstand ye many Temptations you will be exposed to: so abandoned will you find most men as to be ashamed of even appearing virtuous. I do not desire to seclude you from Society or innocent pleasures, but I advise you to be very circumspect in ye choice of your Company, and to watch so that your amusements may not have any ill tendency. Relaxation is even necessary not only to your health, but to a proper prosecution of your Studies.[92]

Charley's father concluded by assuring his son that, "Your Mother and I offer our daily prayers to ye God of Mercies to avert all Dangers from you, to grant you health and every other blessing."[93] Charley lost no time in replying:

> Advice is necessary but most of all a sufficient resolution to put good advice in execution ... Young person's passions are strong of themselves & need no outward encouragement; but when roused by occasions, strengthened by example, fired with wine and Jovial company, become almost irresistible. Tis therefore with the greatest prudence and forecast you recommend to me the choice of my company, a matter really difficult in London, but most so among young men ... That the greatest resolution, prudence & virtue are requisite to protect me from ... contagion is undoubted ... I never like to promise unless morally certain of being able to fulfill my promise: and who can promise to others even to himself to remain

[92] Charles Carroll of Annapolis to Charles Carroll of Carrollton, October 6, 1759, in Thomas Meagher Field, *Unpublished Letters of Charles Carrollton and of His Father, Charles Carroll of Doughoregan* (New York: United States Catholic Historical Society, 1902), 32–33.

[93] Ibid., 35.

> virtuous. I am now in an open sea, hitherto I have rode triumphantly.[94]

While a student at the Inner Temple, Charley had quarters engaged for him by a Mr. Perkins, a merchant of London, and shipowner as well. It appears Perkins served as a sort of guardian for young Carroll during his London student life.

An episode well worth recounting deals with a young (seventeen years of age) English Catholic girl, Louisa Baker, whom Charley had initially been introduced to in Paris by Fr. Alexander Crookshanks, the dear friend of the Carrolls, and procurator of the Jesuit mission in England and Scotland, and whom he was intent on marrying. Louisa was the daughter of John Baker, a wealthy West Indian planter, who, when in England, divided his time between his home in Twickenham, on the outskirts of London, and his country residence, Grove Place, near Southampton. By Charley's much later admission, Louisa was a very beautiful girl, but early on, he described her to his father as "an agreeable person and good natured," a girl whose "temper and amiable qualities" were very attractive. He confided to Charles of Annapolis that he intended to marry Louisa, "Provided I can obtain the Father's & the daughter's consent"; this being accomplished, he quite candidly added, "I flatter myself you can have no objection to the match."[95]

Louisa's parents were much a part of the more affluent English Catholics of their day, by now able to move more freely in British society, with less overt hostility directed at them by the Protestant culture. The question that loomed

[94] Charles Carroll of Carrollton to Charles Carroll of Annapolis, January 29, 1760, cited in Smith, 47.

[95] Charles Carroll of Carrollton to Charles Carroll of Annapolis, October 3, 1763, cited in Hoffman and Mason, 176.

large in Charley's mind was whether the Bakers would want their daughter to leave the very genteel life to which she was accustomed[96] and settle in the frontier of Maryland. Yet another concern was his fear that her parents thought her too young to marry. Charley and Louisa's father seemed to hit it off quite well, and the young man was invited to spend time with the family at Grove Place.

Charles of Annapolis, while somewhat concerned with qualities like character, personality, family background, and so on, seems to have concentrated far more time on financial considerations. He authorized his son to "pledge only the properties that would be bestowed upon him when he returned to Maryland: the 12,700 acre Carrollton manor from whose tenants 250 [pound] sterling was annually realized and a one-fifth share in the Baltimore Company iron works that currently brought in … 400 [pounds] each year."[97] What John Baker's feelings about a proposed marriage was are not clear; he may well have shared those of his wife, whose opinions were the very one's Charley had feared. He confided his pessimism to his father, that he had begun to think "I shall not succeed with miss Baker," adding that "for young ladies the going to America is a prodigious objection."[98] Charley never lost the memory of this young woman—he carried it well into his mature years, and at least one biographer has questioned why such an episode became indelible in his mind:

> Most obviously his inability to win her denied him a sweet moment of triumph. Had he brought home

[96] Louisa was being educated at the Ursuline Convent in Paris.

[97] Hoffman and Mason, 179.

[98] Charles Carroll of Carrollton to Charles Carroll of Annapolis, March 21, 1764, cited in ibid., 180.

> to the colonial periphery an English wife of genteel birth and some fortune, his achievement would have made a significant impression upon the Chesapeake gentry, Protestants as well as Catholics, and earned the colonial Carrolls similar respect and recognition in the mother country as well.[99]

Perhaps one reason for Charley's attraction to Louisa, his desire to settle down and have a family, and the like, was the death of his mother a few years earlier. Though he did not hear of his mother's passing until June of 1761, she had died on March 12, following an illness and the best efforts of several doctors to save her. The young man was devastated—it was the first major emotional crisis he had to face in life, and his grief was added to by the fact that, living in London, he was among practically no one who had known his mother. Keeping his own private grief was doubly difficult, and in his earliest missive to his father, he "poured out his feelings ... asking for the details of his mother's last illness, begging to know if she had mentioned him."[100] His father reminded him that they would find solace and consolation only in their faith—the faithful Christian totally receptive to God's will in all circumstances would receive "that ease which nothing else can give him."[101]

Still another event which pressed heavily on Charley's thinking and emotions was the expulsion of the Jesuits from France in 1762. A plot of sorts was concocted by Jansenists, Gallicans, *philosophes*, and Freemasons—based, among other things, on built-up fears in light of the government of

[99] Ibid., 182.

[100] Smith, 51.

[101] Charles Carroll of Annapolis to Charles Carroll of Carrollton, March 22, 1761, cited in Hoffman and Mason, 165.

Portugal's similar expulsion three years earlier on accusations that Jesuits were plotting to assassinate the king. These were the religious Society who had educated Charley at St. Omer, Rheims, Paris, and Brouges, and in so many ways made him the Catholic gentleman he had become. His father left no doubt where he stood:

> I see how severely ye Jesuits have been handled by ye Parliament of Paris; particular Members of that Society may be indiscreet, they may be wicked—Judas was numbered among ye 12. But is it not inconsistent with ye Rules of Justice ... this, if ye body should not be liable to ye Contracts of Individuals in a [business?] transaction, because it is ye Body that is trusted, as Individuals are known to have no property. But ye Parliament seems to me to have exceeded ye Bounds of their Jurisdiction in censuring ye opinions of their Authors, which I should think only fall properly under ye Cognizance of an Ecclesiastical Tribunal: moreover, what may not any author be made to say if particular propositions or sentences be extracted from his writings without paying a just regard to ye whole Tenor of his Doctrine? Is it not by such means that every Sect of Christians adapt ye scriptures to their opinions? And are not those sacred oracles made to countenance ye most impious and blasphemous Doctrines?[102]

Charley, for his part, studied the Jesuit Constitutions and was amazed they placed far more emphasis on obedience than reason. He accused the Jesuits of "a blind impetuosity of will & eagerness to obey without the least enquiry or examination." He freely admitted admiring their virtue and

[102] Charles Carroll of Annapolis to Charles Carroll of Carrollton, April 8, 1762, cited in Field, 65.

esteeming their learning, but nonetheless their constitutions were "contrary to the true spirit & discipline of the Catholic church."[103] The budding young revolutionary felt that the Jesuit educators would be replaced by "men of republican principles who will not fail to inspire the youth with the love of liberty," though he was also very critical of French parliamentary action in driving the Society from the Eldest Daughter of the Church, as he deplored "the injustice, violence & precipitancy in their proceedings," lamenting at the same time that, "The name of liberty as well as of religion, has often covered the worst designs."[104]

Charley put his well-developed habits of study to work for him in the Inner Temple, and this particular academic course stirred some interesting inner thoughts which he shared with his father. He seemed, initially, to have difficulty securing one individual who would be adept at instructing him in the law, one on one. He felt the best way to become a good lawyer is to be under one, not as his clerk, but to be in his law office "on the footing of a gentleman by allowing him handsome gratification." It would give him a practical knowledge of the law, while private instruction would provide the intellectual content:

> Nothing can be more absurd than the usual manner of young gentlemen's studying the law. They come from the University, take chambers in the Temple, read Coke Little: whom they cannot possibly understand, frequent the courts, whose practice they are ignorant of; they are soon disgusted with the difficulties and

[103] Charles Carroll of Carrollton to Charles Carroll of Annapolis, October 22, 1761, cited in McDermott, 48.

[104] Charles Carroll of Carrollton to Charles Carroll of Annapolis, June 14, 1763, cited in ibid., 49.

> dryness of the study, the law books are thrown aside, dissipation succeeds to study, immorality to virtue, one night plunges them in ruin, misery and disease.[105]

The letter may serve more as an assessment of Charley's own mind than a mere passing observation on many with whom he studied. He never envisioned the practice of law becoming possible once back in Maryland, primarily because his religious faith precluded it, and one could easily form the conclusion he felt much more of it to be time wasting. Charles of Annapolis, however, did not see it in quite the same way:

> I have always told you I never intended you should practice ye law; will, therefore, ye knowledge of it be unprofitable to you? Would it not be of infinite advantage to England if every man of property who serves in Parliament were a sound Lawyer and well acquainted with the Constitution? ... Will it not enable you to state your own Cases, to instruct those you employ; and, if you find them ignorant, knavish or conceited, direct you to employ others? It is true, I have met with some of these Characters, but had I been a Lawyer, or deemed such, it's more than probable they would not have ventured to have imposed on me.[106]

One cannot be away from home for seventeen years without expecting, and indeed seeing, much change upon return. Charley's came at the exact time when great political tension was about to translate into colonial action. The year 1763

[105] Charles Carroll of Carrollton to Charles Carroll of Annapolis, January 7, 1863, cited in Rowland, 1, 53–54. Coke Little was an early commentator on British law.

[106] Charles Carroll of Annapolis to Charles Carroll of Carrollton, December 29, 1762, cited in Smith, 52–53. See also Field, 75–76.

has always been considered the beginning of the era of the American Revolution. Maryland and all the other colonies were caught up in political events that would profoundly affect their future and in political sentiments that quickly snowballed to the point of no return.

By 1763, England was the most powerful nation in the world. In order to hold this power together, it had to begin tightening the reins. The national debt had increased to 130 million pounds and the general expenses of running the government multiplied threefold. Land taxes were raised throughout the empire, and the decision was made to station an army in America to safeguard their territory from Indian attacks and invasions from French Canada. All these factors combined to force English officials to wonder: if costs are so high, why should not the colonies pay their fair share? Americans, on the other hand, were already paying church taxes, colonial taxes, and certain imperial taxes; they could not understand why these revenues were not sufficient.

By the spring of 1763, the government in London was seriously studying the question of further taxing the colonists. The Treasury board set up commissioners to regulate the customs service in America. These individuals, known as the British Board of Customs Commissioners (BBC), were not cabinet rank; rather, policy was set by the Treasury board and carried out by the commissioners. The BBC related to Treasury that existing laws were being flagrantly violated and recommended that the customs service should be reorganized for more efficiency and effectiveness. All customs officers were ordered to their posts throughout the empire, and many additional officials such as collectors, controllers, surveyors, tide waiters, land waiters, and so on were appointed. The

BBC sent a letter to all colonial governors telling them to enforce the laws or there would be serious consequences.

In the spring of 1764, Prime Minister George Grenville's government introduced the Sugar Act, a very high tax on rum and molasses, and a complete reversal of British economic thinking. The act cut in half the import duty on foreign molasses but provided for strict enforcement; the government wanted to increase revenues and strengthen the already existing Navigation Acts.[107] The old tax was designed to stamp out foreign trade entirely; this one, however, was the first purely revenue-raising tax in the history of the mother country's relationship with her colonies. It was also the first piece of legislation shifting Britain from a mercantile to an imperial system. The mercantile system had been designed to protect merchants, farmers, and manufacturers and was based on the idea that government control would help these stakeholders. Under the imperial system, the government was simply trying to maximize revenue. No clearance could be given to ships going to England unless the entire cargo was headed there; every accusation against a vessel was to be tried in admiralty courts, and the burden of proof was on the owner.

The Sugar Act, as well might be imagined, generated objections, protests and petitions, especially from New England and New York, whose markets were hardest hit. Opposition was still only local and sporadic, but opponents of the London regime began working on constitutional themes that in a few years would be fully developed arguments. The same year, the Currency Act forbade bills of

[107] The Navigation Acts (1651, 1660) were acts of Parliament intended to promote the self-sufficiency of the British Empire by restricting colonial trade to England and decreasing dependence on foreign imported goods.

credit as legal tender. Any governor approving such bills would be fined one thousand pounds and forced to leave office. This act was very unpopular since it forbade any substitution for hard money.

In 1765, the Stamp Act was the first attempt to solve the problem of liberty and order in the relationship between the colonists and the mother country. It also emerged because Britain had accumulated an enormous debt and a vast empire. Stamp taxes, which required certain paper products to be produced on special stamp paper, were very much the vogue in England, and some of the colonies themselves had moderate stamp taxes. By May 1764, Grenville was already signaling that he had no intention of allowing the colonies to tax themselves, as some felt he should; he insisted on a tax levied by Parliament and sent a letter to all colonial governors, asking for a list of what could legitimately be taxed. The legal argument was whether Parliament had the right to levy a tax on internal commerce among the colonies, since, in 1765, all the colonies were not royal ones. Meanwhile, colonials living in England immediately began applying for positions as stamp collectors at home—not even beginning to realize how much opposition the act would engender.

The stamp tax would take effect on November 1, 1765, and was imposed on legal and commercial documents, wills, deeds, licenses, leases, mortgages, bonds, insurance policies, playing cards, advertisements, newspapers, magazines, and the like. The tax was to be collected in specie—that is, gold or silver—not local currency. All offenders were to be tried in the admiralty courts, since these had no juries. Money from the tax was to be spent in the colonies, and all stamps were provided by England. The government hoped to raise sixty thousand pounds, but before any money was collected, an organized opposition developed: the more literate upper classes seethed, and colonial newspapers were full of condemnatory editorials.

As tensions continued to mount, Charley kept in close touch with some of his fellow legal students in London. One of these was Edward Jennings, a fellow Marylander whose interest in affairs would have been equal to Carroll's. In September of 1765, he confided to his friend that the Stamp Act "continues to make as much noise as ever," adding that "the spirit of discontent in the people rather continues to increase than diminish." He went on to say that the Maryland stamp collector, one Zacharia Hood, is "hated and despised by everyone; he has been whipped, pilloried and hanged in effigy ... the people seem determined not to buy his goods."[108] Some weeks later, he further confided that if the Stamp Act should be enforced by "tyrannical soldiery, our property, our liberty, our very existence is at an end."[109]

> Nothing can overcome the aversion of the people to the Stamp Act, and [overcome] their love of liberty, but an armed force; and that, too, not a contemptible one. To judge from the number of the colonists, and the spirit they have already shown, and which I hope to God will not fail them on the day of trial, twenty thousand men would find it difficult to enforce the law; or more properly speaking to ram it down our throats. Can England, surrounded with powerful enemies, distracted with intestine factions, encumbered, and almost staggering under the immense load of debt—little short of one hundred and fifty million pounds—send out

[108] Charles Carroll of Carrollton to Edward Jennings, September 5, 1765, cited in Rowland, 1, 73.

[109] Ibid., September 28, 1765, cited in ibid.

> such a powerful army to deprive a free people, their fellow subjects of their rights and liberties? If ministerial influence and parliamentary corruption should not blush at such a detestable scheme; if Parliament, blind to their own interest, and forgetting that they are the guardians of sacred liberty, and of our happy constitution, should have the impudence to avow this open infraction of both, will England, her commerce annihilated by the oppression of America, be able to maintain those troops?

The letter's continuation offers a unique view of the times:

> At a moderate computation, the inhabitants of these continental colonies amount to two million, five hundred thousand; and in twenty years time as propagation increases in proportion to the means of an easy subsistence, the number will be doubled. Reflect on the immense ocean that divides this fruitful country from the island whose power, as its territory is circumscribed, has already arrived at its zenith, while the power of this continent is growing daily, and in time will be as unbounded as our dominions are extensive. The rapid increase of manufactures surpasses the expectations of the most sanguine American. Even the arts and sciences commence to flourish, and in these, as in arms, the day, I hope, will come when America will be superior to all the world. Without prejudice or partiality, I do not believe the universe can show a finer country—so luxuriant in its soil; so happy in a healthy climate; so extensively watered by so many navigable rivers, and producing within itself not only all the necessaries, but even most of the superfluities of life ...
>
> Many imagine the Stamp Act will be suspended for a time, till some expedient may be hit on to reconcile

> the exemption we claim from a parliamentary taxation, with the right and power asserted of late by the Parliament. If the act be suspended until such an expedient can be found, it will be suspended for all eternity.[110]

Things were to move in a different direction than Charley had predicted. The most significant protest was the Stamp Act Congress, which met in New York City in October 1765. Three petitions were drawn up: to the king, to the House of Lords, and to the House of Commons. It was too late to set up an effective boycott, so the emphasis was on opposition to the stamp collectors. Some, as Carroll had indicated of Maryland, were hanged in effigy, while others suffered significant damage to their properties. Nonimportation associations sprang up throughout the colonies, declaring that there would be no importation of colonial goods until the Stamp Act was repealed—and the Sugar Act modified, for good measure. This developed into a unified, well-enforced boycott that was felt in England. Although the militant Sons of Liberty played an important role in the agitation and protest in each colony, at this point not even the most radical protestors spoke of independence.

After Grenville's deteriorating political situation compelled him to resign, Lord Rockingham formed his new government. By March 1766, London had repealed the Stamp Act and modified the Sugar Act—but at the same time passed the Declaratory Act, which stated that Parliament had the right to regulate for the colonies in all cases whatsoever. Some have seen this as a statement of strength developed to save face after acceding to the colonists' demands, but in fact, for years there had been

[110] Ibid., September 30, 1765, cited in ibid., 74–75.

pressure within the British government to make such a declaration to put the colonists on notice.

The events surrounding the Stamp Act proved to be a unifying force in the colonies, leading to the development of a more sophisticated form of constitutional argumentation. The Congress in New York has been described as a monument to colonial initiative and a moment of unique colonial unity. The atmosphere was made more tense by the passage of the Quartering Act, affecting New York and Halifax, Nova Scotia, which strongly asserted what colonists had to supply to troops living in their colonies.

In the summer of 1766, Charley wrote to William Graves, a good friend, and a master in Chancery—one of those clerks who assist the Chancellor of a Court of Chancery in various duties:

> The colonies are far from aiming at independence. If, indeed, slavery and dependency be convertible terms—and if your government should not make the proper distinction, and should treat us, not as culprits composing a part of the same society, and entitled to the same privileges with the rest, but should look upon us as slaves, and should use us as such, I believe every American would disclaim that sort of dependency.[111]

Rockingham's government fell in the same month as Carroll wrote to Graves, and it was replaced by that of William Pitt, Earl of Chatham, and Augustus FitzRoy, Duke of Grafton. During this time, Charles Townsend became Chancellor of

[111] Charles Carroll of Carrollton to William Graves, August 12, 1766, cited in ibid., 75–76.

the Exchequer[112] and proceeded to institute his now famous duties. Upon Pitt's retirement, Grafton was not up to the task of governing, and Townsend assumed leadership by default; he had always been an ally of former Prime Minister Grenville, mutually agreeing that the American colonies must pay their way. Hence, there would be new custom duties designed to pay for the existence of all colonial officials, and America was to receive its own board of customs commissioners. This American Board of Customs Commissioners (ABC) represented, in the minds of many historians, the point of no return for the American colonies.[113]

The ABC was independent of all colonial governors—and let them know it. They controlled all thirty-two ports, including Bermuda and the Bahamas, and their headquarters were in Boston. They reorganized the customs service, increased the number of lesser offices, and, at one point, wanted to build a coast guard. Had their headquarters been elsewhere than Boston, already a center of opposition to parliamentary authority, there might not have been a revolution.

The commissioners set up a system of General Letters, sent to each of the individual ports, along with a detailed questionnaire asking for very specific details about their operations. They had inspectors general and an enormous bureaucracy, establishing an elaborate system of books, reports, and so on. Every port was given a copy of everyone else's seal for authenticity, and officials in England who discovered smuggling were instructed to write ahead to warn officials in America. The ABC sent details to the home government, especially noting Boston as a hotbed of rebellion; as

[112] Similar to today's American Secretary of the Treasury.

[113] Its members were: Robinson, Hulton, Burch, Paxton, and Temple.

a result, troops were sent to Boston for the express purpose of putting down any possible revolt.

The ABC tried often to secure writs of assistance, allowing customs officials to search premises for illicit goods, but American courts would not comply; England told them these orders were legal, but, for the most part, courts continued to refuse. The new dispensation increased revenue, taking in thirty thousand pounds annually against thirteen thousand in costs—but at the cost of losing the colonies themselves.

The Townsend Acts became law in 1767. They were enacted on the colonies solely to raise revenue: taxes were levied on paper, glass, painter's colors, and tea. This was seen as an attempt to undermine the authority of the colonial assemblies; it was a complete abandonment of the mother country's previous mercantile policy. There was not the unified opposition there had been to the Stamp Act, but criticisms were raised in the publication of John Dickinson's *Letters from a Farmer in Pennsylvania, to the Inhabitants of the British Colonies*, as well as the *Massachusetts Circular Letter*. Dickinson admitted Parliament's right to regulate trade but denied its right to tax to raise revenue in America; Sam Adams, author of the second document, denounced the duties as violating the principle of no taxation without representation.[114] These two strong statements, along with a program for austerity, all contributed to a powerful uniting of the colonies.

Clashes between citizens and soldiers were not uncommon, especially in Boston where so much resistance was to be

[114] This principle underscored the colonists' belief in the unfairness of not being physically represented in the British Parliament; the mother country would respond with the concept of virtual representation, that all British subjects, regardless of where they were to be geographically found, were represented in Parliament.

found. The Boston Massacre of March 1770, killing three outright and wounding two others mortally, was to have lasting repercussions and fell short of a general uprising only when American patriot Sam Adams demanded the colonial government withdraw its troops from the town to islands in the harbor.

The colonial nonimportation boycott was quite successful; imports dropped one million pounds in one year. Further, revenue from the Townsend Acts did not measure up to the expected forty thousand pounds, producing only slightly more than half that figure. Townsend himself had died in September 1767 and was succeeded by Lord North as Chancellor of the Exchequer. King George III established personal rule, in which he took on expanded authority and responsibility in the parliamentary structure, and he set up a ministry that was to be led by North. In the spring of 1770, all the Townsend duties were repealed—except the tax on tea, which was kept purely to maintain the principle that Parliament had the right to legislate in the colonies.

The period from 1771 to 1773 was one of peace and prosperity—the lull before the storm. Colonial merchants seemed quite happy. Meanwhile, though, the always plotting Sam Adams was setting up committees of correspondence to organize further opposition to London, though it is not certain if even he was thinking in terms of independence at this point. The purpose of the committees was simply to provide information and to ensure cooperation among the colonies.

In May 1773, Parliament passed the Tea Act, not so much to generate revenue as to save the British East India Company—specifically to enable tea dealers to undersell smugglers. The company had to be rescued because of its corrupt and inefficient management; they paid high dividends but at the same time owed great debts to the British government. Many members of Parliament were shareholders, and a general panic was feared if the company went under. The British continued, of course, to export their tea to colonial ports, but the act imposed barriers to non-East India Company importation. When one East India Company ship, eventually joined by two others, came into the Port of Boston and refused to turn back, the Sons of Liberty organized the famed Boston Tea Party, dumping some ninety thousand pounds of tea into the Charles River on the night of December 16, 1773. When the news reached England, the Boston Port Bill immediately became law, closing the city's port until the tea was paid for. In addition, a further bill was passed changing the colonial charter: the governor was to appoint and remove all judges, jurors were to be picked by sheriffs, and there were to be no town meetings. A third act passed, dealing with unfair trials, and a new quartering act brought additional troops to the city. Once again, this legislation served as a tremendous unifier of the colonists.

There seemed to occur at this point a total transformation of American society:

> Among those who were opposed to extreme measures were the conservatives, British or colonial born, men who were actuated by sentiment rather than principle, were loyal to their oath of allegiance to the King and sincerely believed in the existing constitutional order. They represented all grades of society, rich and poor alike; some held office under the Crown and some contented themselves with private life. Second, there were the merchants and other members of the propertied class … whose instincts were conservative, and whose preferences, little influenced by questions of

political and constitutional theory, were for friendly cooperation with their fellow merchants of Great Britain in order to preserve a business connection that was profitable to all. Thirdly, there were those, neither bold enough nor reckless enough to court disaster, who opposed a declaration of independence, because they believed that an armed contest with Great Britain would end in defeat and the consequent ruin of the colonies. Among members of all these groups were thousands who were patriotic at heart and devoted to America, whose moderate views were due not to moral cowardice or self-interest only, but to honest convictions and a natural instinct of self-preservation. At the other extreme were the radicals, many of whom ... had banded together as Sons of Liberty. At first these groups were composed of moderates and radicals alike, but later, as the movement advanced, only radicals remained, young and fiery souls with none too much respect for constituted authority and intensely antagonistic to all phases of British policy ... Many of the more temperate among them were high-minded, well-educated thoughtful men who ... raised the issue from a mere dispute about money to the dignity of a cosmic event. Others ... were radical by nature, and willing to sacrifice even their property interests for a cause in which they profoundly believed and which they upheld with a vociferousness that often bordered on hysteria ... Still others were born political agitators, gifted with a genius for persuasion, propaganda and organization ... Last of all were those whom the conservatives called the inferior sort, the populace, or the mob, to many of whom the colonists had never granted the right to vote, who bore few of the responsibilities of citizenship, paid a minimum of taxes and were without

> property or civic obligations ... They were the terrorists of the period, many of whom did their thinking with their muscles ... Their influence lay in their physical ability to override law and order, destroy property and intimidate their enemies.[115]

Much of this description of American society changed drastically in light of the events just described. The First Continental Congress, held in Philadelphia, was the first in a series of steps in the colonial attempt to bring about liberty and order. Catholics, no more than their fellow colonists, were acutely aware of political developments in the decades preceding the revolution, and their subsequent response can be understood only in light of this background.

115 Charles M. Andrews, *The Colonial Background of the American Revolution* (New Haven: Yale University Press, 1924), 146–148.

CHAPTER 3

AN AMERICAN PATRIOT EMERGES

In mid-February 1765, after seventeen years of study, incultura-tion, and growth in his Catholic Faith, Charles Carroll arrived back in his native Maryland. He first went to his father's house in Annapolis, and, as the elder Carroll had previously arranged, his son was given the ten-thousand-acre manor of Carrollton in Fredrick County, from which he took the title which distinguished him for the remainder of his life. Maryland's capital city in 1765 had arrived at what one prominent diarist called its "golden age," and was:

> A gay little town with a polished and affluent society. The fine houses and splendid horses and carriages attested to the wealth of upper class Annapolitans whose frequent and sumptuous amusements seemed so profuse at times that [the diarist] wondered how pocketbooks and health could stand them! In addition to the balls, dinners and performances staged purely for the social elite by such exclusive groups as the Maryland Jockey Club, the Governor, in order

> to increase his popularity, frequently financed public balls and provided purses for horse races.[116]

Charles Carroll never lived permanently at Carrollton but did erect a manor house where he spent days or weeks at a time. It was about a day's travel from his other estates at Annapolis or Doughoregan Manor in Ellicott City, where in later years he would make his permanent home. He also built a farm called Tuscarora on Carrollton Manor where he made his headquarters while overseeing the estate. In addition, houses were built on the Manor for his slaves and his overseers, giving it the appearance of a small community. Perhaps a significant manifestation of his Catholic Faith came with his gift of land on the Manor for the erection of a church dedicated to St. Joseph, to this day located in Buckeystown, and a flourishing parish.

> Here Charles Carroll of Carrollton gave the land for the church and graveyard. The location for the church is another evidence of the splendid foresight of Mr. Carroll in supplying a place of worship for the faithful as convenient to them as it was possible to make it. The church originally built of limestone, faced the east and west with the entrance to the west ... Catholics from Virginia and the southern end of Fredrick County came many miles to Mass bringing their lunch with them.[117]

116 Van Devanter, 25. The diarist in question was William Eddis, secretary to Maryland's Royal Governor Robert Eden.

117 William Jarboe Grove, *History of Carrollton Manor, Fredrick County, Md* (Lime Kiln, Maryland: 1922), 7. The church was later rebuilt after the Civil War, and Grove notes the painting of Christ Crucified over the main altar, purchased in Rome by Emily Caton MacTavish, Carroll's granddaughter. All other paintings were described as "masterpieces done by a Fredrick

Not home for more than a year, it seemed marriage was on the horizon, this time to a Miss Rachel Cooke. Of a staunch Catholic family, she was the daughter of John and Sophia Sewall Cooke, her father being a Prince George's County planter. Her mother and Charley's maternal grandmother, Jane Sewall Brooke, had been sisters, making he and Rachel first cousins once removed. The family lived at Graiden, some twenty-two miles from Annapolis. Charley and Rachel received "from the Jesuit superior in Maryland, the waiver of consanguinity required for a valid union between closely related cousins."[118] The wedding was set for the summer of 1766, but Charley came down with a serious fever, causing its postponement until November. While all seemed in readiness, the bride-to-be, in turn, came down with a far more serious malady. Charley visited her every day and was present at her death on November 25, 1766. The natural shock he experienced was doubled by the fact of his not being sufficiently forewarned of the nature of her condition. Young hopes were dashed, and the soon-to-be statesman wrote that:

County artist, Miss Gertrude Stemer," ibid., 8. Emily MacTavish was the daughter of Carroll's daughter Mary and her husband Richard Caton. Described as Carroll's favorite granddaughter, Fr. John M. Chanche, a family friend, noted that at the end of his life, the Signer "remarked that he wished to protect ... all his gifts to Mrs. MacTavish, as he did not wish to get his affairs into the hands of the lawyers as they would afford them fine pickings." Fr. Chanche also related that, "Not one of the members of the other branches of the family" took such care of the old man as Mrs. MacTavish did; also, he was especially fond of her husband [John MacTavish], a Scotchman who had been sent from Canada as consul to the port of Baltimore. John MacTavish was one of those to whom, in his extreme old age, Charles Carroll issued a power of attorney." Smith, n. 29; 304.

118 Hoffman and Mason, 197.

> The young lady to whom I was to have been married died on the 25th Instant. She was acknowledged by all her acquaintance, to be a most sweet tempered, amiable & virtuous girl: I loved her most sincerely & and had all reason to believe I was sincerely loved — Judge of my loss & and by it of what I now feel — but I must drop this melancholy subject; my heart is too full & and my mind is at present too decomposed, to permit me to be as full & circumstantial as usual.[119]

Although his personal life was deeply saddened, Charley was by no means living in isolation or turned in upon himself; on the contrary, since his return from Europe, he had closely followed political developments, especially in the aftermath of the Stamp Act of 1765 and the tremendous dissention it produced.

Writing to a friend in England in the fall of 1765, Carroll was acutely aware that trouble loomed; at the same time, he was not of the mentality that any break from the mother country was part of the foreseeable landscape:

> The climate here is delightful—particularly ye Autumn: the weather is now as mild and serene as it generally is in England in August and September: many who have traveled through the colonies give ye preference to Maryland, both in point of climate, ye fertility of its soil, and ye sociability of its inhabitants. As the English Constitution seems hastening to its final period of dissolution, and the symptoms of a general decay are but too visible, I advise you to sell your estate in England and to purchase lands in this province where liberty will maintain her empire, till a dissoluteness of morals, luxury and venality shall have prepared the

[119] Charles Carroll of Carrollton to William Graves, October 15, 1766, cited in ibid., 198.

> degenerate sons of some future age, to prefer their own mean lucre, ye bribes, and the smiles of corruption and arbitrary ministers, to patriotism, to glory, and to ye publik weal—no doubt the same causes will produce the same effects and a period is already set to ye reign of American freedom; but that fatal time seems to be at a great distance—the present generation at least, and I hope many succeeding ones, in spite of a corrupt Parliament, will enjoy the blessings of ye sweets of liberty.[120]

For now, at least, only immediate problems were of concern. He confided to his lawyer friend and fellow Marylander now living in England, Edmund Jennings, that merchants in both New York and Philadelphia had come to a resolution "not to send for any more goods of ye manufacture and growth of Great Britain, and to contradict the orders already given, till a repeal of ye Stamp Act is obtained," adding that "this resolution will in my opinion avail us more than petitioning."[121] Less than two weeks following his correspondence with Jennings, Charley's rhetoric was even more pronounced in what he inferred from the colonial retaliation against the Stamp Act:

> The Americans are jealous of their privileges and resolved to maintain them: they are not yet corrupt enough to undervalue Liberty, they are truly sensible of its blessings, and not only talk of them as they do somewhere else, but really wish their continuance—they think the most effectual method of obtaining redress against oppression is to make the oppressors feel it: the ready way to do this is to distress

[120] Charles Carroll of Carrollton to Thomas Bradshaw, November 21, 1765, Field, 97.

[121] Charles Carroll of Carrollton to Edmund Jennings, November 23, 1765, ibid., 99–100.

> the merchants, shopkeepers, tradesmen and manufacturers of England.[122]

At Christmas, Carroll believed his own area, Fredrick County, Maryland, would follow the same course as so much of the eastern seaboard was doing, noting that "the Fredric county court has obliged their clerk to issue writs as usual: Baltimore, it is said, will do ye same—and this conduct, in my apprehension, is but rational and a necessary consequence, if the people would act consequentially, of what they have already done."[123]

Chapters of the Sons of Liberty quickly spread from New York to the other colonies, a testimony to the uniformity of sentiment rapidly growing. Maryland's chapter merited Charley's full approval, and he very accurately predicted the Stamp Act's repeal in 1766 some time before it occurred:

> Many imagine the Act will be suspended for a time, till some expedient may be hit on to reconcile ye exemption we claim from a Parliamentary taxation, with that right and power so impolitically asserted of late by ye Parliament: if the Act should be suspended till such an expedient can be found out, it will be suspended for all eternity: unless indeed the Parliament should be content with resolving they have such a right and never attempt to carry it into execution; but in that case, it is more probable that on passing this resolve, they will repeal the Stamp Act: since the leaving that odious law suspended and hanging over our heads, like an immense ruin ready to fall and crush us to atoms by

[122] Charles Carroll of Carrollton to Thomas Bradshaw, December 8, 1765, ibid., 101–102.

[123] Charles Carroll of Carrollton to Daniel Barrington, December 22, 1765, cited in ibid., 104.

> its weight, will only increase ye apprehensions and ill humor of the colonists, and confirm in them a habit of industry and manufacturing which nothing but oppression could have lead them into and perhaps nothing but a prospect of the same returning upon them once more, will be able to keep up.[124]

Opposition to the Stamp Act on the part of the American colonists has been carefully studied by countless political historians, and such resistance, by general agreement, is categorized in three groups. There were those who were opposed on principle; to many it seemed unconstitutional, an act bordering on tyranny on the part of the King-in-Parliament. As these people looked at English common law, not to mention their own colonial charters, they saw an infringement of their rights which necessitated a very strong response. These people might be described as intellectual idealists, and surely had their sympathizers in England as well as on their own turf.[125] Then there were those whose opposition stemmed from economic rather than political motives. These would be merchants, owners of newspapers, lawyers, and so on, for whom the tax would impose significant financial hardship. Finally, there was a class of citizens for whom the particulars of the Stamp Act were of little consequence but saw its imposition as cause for rebellion; those who were economically deprived and may perhaps have seen a break from the mother country, whatever form it would take, as a means of improving their lot in life. Within this third group were yet another minority, one especially well represented in Maryland. These

[124] Charles Carroll of Carrollton to Daniel Barrington, March 17, 1766, cited in ibid., 109–110.

[125] William Pitt and Edmund Burke were significant examples in the mother country.

were individuals, largely if not exclusively Scottish, who had stood by the Stuart monarchy for decades and came to the defense of the young pretender, Charles Edward Stuart, when he made his final attempt to regain the throne at the Battle of Culloden in Scotland in April 1746. These individuals, legally British subjects, did not consider themselves English whatsoever. The same could be said of the Irish, of whom the Carroll family serve as excellent examples.

> All the Carrolls felt very strongly about being Irish. The Attorney-General, the only one who could claim the Sod as his birthplace, was extremely anxious that his children should never forget their heritage. When his boys were at school at St. Omer he wrote instructing them to sign their theses "Marylando-Hibernus." His son, Charles Carroll of Annapolis, was many years later still conscious of 'ye duty all Irishmen owe to ye Glory and Honour of their Country.' His grandson, as a young student planning a tour of Europe deliberately left Ireland out of his itinerary: 'The present situation of that [Island], will only renew the memory of past wrongs.' He had been thoroughly educated in the family tradition ... His opinion of the English government was, even more than he himself realized, as hereditary as his high-bridged nose. He was a born fighter, a born crusader, a born rebel—in a word, he was an Irishman. Hatred of political England had been bred into him ... he had wanted passionately to be, some day, free of the oppression which English rule had meant to his people. He saw the Stamp Act controversy, clear-eyed, as an opening wedge.[126]

In August 1767, Charley confided to a friend in England he was soon to be married to a cousin, Mary (Molly) Darnall.

[126] Smith, 77–78.

By the time the future Signer had returned to America, Molly had been resident in the Carroll household for some four years. Her grandfather, Henry Darnall III, had a reputation for years of living beyond his means; this had brought his family into financial ruin, and Charles Carroll of Annapolis had to some extent salvaged him by securing for him a position as Naval Officer of the Patuxent. True to form, however, Darnall was caught embezzling huge sums from the public till and was immediately removed from office. Shortly after, Darnall and his eldest son, Henry Jr. (Molly's father), signed an indenture forfeiting their rights to their once sizeable fortune. He fled to Europe, where he lived on the brink of poverty for years; the career of his son remains very obscure, but his daughter Molly was taken in by the Carroll family and made her home with them until her marriage to Charles of Carrollton. Their marriage was blessed with a number of children, though only three survived to adulthood:

> The first baby, a daughter named Elizabeth after Carroll's mother, was born in 1766 and lived less than a year. Six more pregnancies followed in rapid succession, and by 1780, Molly had born seven children and buried three—her first, her third, Louisa Rachel, and her fifth, Anne. Her last baby, named Eliza, born in 1780, survived her by only a year. The second child, 'Little Pol,' as her doting grandfather called her, was born in September, 1770, and became her father's favorite. In 1775, the long-desired son and heir, another Charles Carroll, later called of Homewood, arrived, 'ye finest Boy in the world, as Molly says to her Mama!' Catherine, nicknamed

> Kitty, the third Carroll child who lived to maturity, was born in 1778.[127]

By now, a revolutionary gentleman was in the making. His social position, European education, family background, and the like all contributed to a natural feeling on the part of his fellow Marylanders that Charley would be their natural selection as a leader in the colony, and, as events were soon to prove, in the new nation. The event setting these things in motion came in 1770 when the Maryland House of Delegates passed a bill regulating officers' fees, as well as prohibiting the sale of offices. In the past, the Colonial Assembly had regulated such fees, but now, the proprietary governor and the Assembly were unable to agree on the proper fee scale; such being the case, the governor took it into his own hands, by official proclamation, to set such fees at the level the Assembly had set seven years earlier. Within the House of Delegates, opposition members began to protest; this was, they felt, another assault on American liberty by the British government, and if left to be, they predicted dire consequences if the government became financially independent of the electorate. Overwhelmingly,

127 Van Devanter, 27. Little Pol later came to be called Mary and married an Englishman, Richard Caton. Their home, at Front and Lombard Streets in Baltimore, was the home in which Charles Carroll died in 1832; Charles Carroll of Homewood married Harriet Chew of Philadelphia, the daughter of the Chief Justice of the Pennsylvania Supreme Court, Benjamin Chew. Long survived by his father, Homewood proved a great disappointment to his father, with his life of debauchery, and was, in the end, refused burial in the Carroll family graveyard at Doughoregan Manor. Catherine, or Kitty, married Robert Goodloe Harper, a leading figure in the Federalist Party in South Carolina.

the delegates voted against the governor's measure, referring to it as "robbery."[128]

Carroll of Annapolis felt that a war, of sorts, had been declared between the people and the government; if such could occur in the Maryland colony, who could predict the consequences of this event, especially coupled with similar situations as they erupted in colony after colony? Within the Colonial Assembly, the opposition quickly came to the forefront, giving themselves the name Independent Whigs. Those who came to the forefront were prominent Marylanders like Samuel Chase, William Paca, and Thomas Johnson; of these, the first two would join Charles Carroll as signers of the Declaration of Independence from their state. Carroll of Annapolis preferred to call these Whigs the Popular Party; though quite conservative in outlook, they also stressed "the concept of republican virtue over the traditional bonds of honor and loyalty that characterized the court party."[129] Carroll of Carrollton was now poised to assume his role as spokesman for the Popular Party and faced off against a rival of long standing—Daniel Dulany, Jr.

The Dulany family had long been adversaries of the Carrolls. Fellow Irish, the former had conformed to the established church, making them all the more acceptable to the proprietary interests, and more likely to be fully accepted by the Maryland Protestant ascendancy.[130]

[128] McDermott, 95.

[129] Ibid., 96. The term *court party*, as used by the author, means to signify those in close alignment with the proprietary interests of the Calvert proprietors and those in government, including Governor Eden himself, who were determined to uphold those interests.

[130] That Protestant ascendancy had come into its own years earlier when Governor Benedict Leonard Calvert left the Faith of his fathers to become an Anglican.

In 1762, studying law in London, Carroll had met Dulany, Jr., and taken an instant dislike to him. Dulany seemed self-important, humorless; "*c'est un homme bizarre*," Carroll wrote his father, whose own low opinion of Dulany grew out of their troubled partnership in the Baltimore ironworks as well as the Dulanys' connection to the all-Protestant court party. Bad blood between the families went back many years. In 1769 Lloyd Dulany had written so maliciously of Carroll of Carrollton's father that the younger man had felt obligated to avenge those words with "a brace of pistols"—an offer Dulany had avoided by dismissing Carroll as a "silly little puppy" and "dirty little rascal" ... The "First Citizen" series helped to coalesce leadership of a new antiproprietary coalition that came to be known as the "popular party" and to bring it victory in the spring election. Reviving the Annapolis-Baltimore alliance, the new network formed around Samuel Chase and the Catholic Carrolls. Carroll of Carrollton's cousin and active supporter, the Annapolis attorney of the same name, had married a daughter of Matthew Tilghman, the Talbot County planter and house speaker. Also on friendly terms with Chase, Carroll the Barrister thus provided a link with two important legislative figures. Thomas Johnson, the anti-Stamp Act leader who served as legal advisor to the Carroll family, and William Cooke, whose sister before her untimely death Carroll of Carrollton had planned to marry, gave the circle around "First Citizen" additional weight. William Paca had read law with Stephen Bordley in Annapolis and briefly at the Inns of Court. A member of the House of Delegates, Paca maintained friendly relations with

> Eden in the early months of 1773 and led the circle news of the governor's activity.[131]

In the course of the newspaper debates which soon began in the *Maryland Gazette*, Carroll of Carrollton assumed the pen-name "First Citizen," and his opponent "Antilon." Both had been liberally educated, both easily defended their positions—one on the part of those who so soon would be fighting for American independence from the mother country, the other who would ultimately embrace loyalism. Carroll, as a continentally educated Catholic, was formed by unique influences and quite representative of his generation:

> It was not surprising ... that their emergence from the great ferment of the French Enlightenment and its reflected glory in England left them quite different in their outlook from what had been the case with their fathers. They would no longer move comfortably in thought and feeling before the sufferance found in the old alliance with the Anglican gentry in the proprietary party. The seventeenth century tradition of freedom took an enlarged meaning for them. As the younger Protestant gentry became critical of the proprietary regime and the restrictions of the imperial government generally, young Catholic intellectuals such as Charles Carroll of Carrolton and John Carroll saw who their new allies were and how the traditional alliance must change. There quietly began an alliance with an anti-proprietary party, composed of men like Samuel Chase, William Paca and

[131] Brugger, 111. Lloyd Dulany was the son of Daniel Dulany Sr. and brother of Daniel Jr. He was killed in a duel in London in 1782. Bordley was a prominent lawyer in Ann Arundel, Prince George's, and Baltimore Counties, who also served in both the lower and upper houses of the Maryland Assembly.

> Thomas Johnson, whose parents had formerly stood with the proprietor's governor against insurgents. It is occasionally stated in the Carroll writings, as well as in those of their Protestant critics, that the young Maryland Catholic's experience with Jesuit schools constituted an education in republicanism. Studies in recent times have brought out liberal features in the Carroll educational environment which interacted with the Enlightenment. What made the process dynamic in the case of the young Carrolls, however, was the fusion of this stream of Catholic thought with their inherited Maryland tradition of freedom. There was consequentially in the minds and hearts of these men an aspiration for a new society just as there was in the case of Chase, Paca and Johnson among the young Protestant revolutionaries. In particular, a natural-rights theory was coupled with Catholic philosophical writings on the legitimacy of revolution, so that active involvement in the movement for independence was spontaneous. There is no doubt that the Catholic gentry saw their religious emancipation as well as their political independence coming to realization in the Declaration of Independence.[132]

And with that intellectual background, the first significant controversy of Carroll of Carrollton's career was about to unfold. Charles of Carrollton officially entered the debate with Dulany on February 4, 1773, in the pages of the *Maryland Gazette*. By all accounts, he came across as witty, a man full of practical wisdom, and even entertaining. He based his argu-

[132] Thomas O'Brien Hanley, S.J., *The American Revolution and Religion: Maryland 1770–1800* (Washington, DC: The Catholic University of America Press, 1971), 175. Hereafter cited as Hanley, *Religion*.

ments throughout on moral and philosophical principles, and relied on relatively recent British and French writers, as well as ancient sources.[133] He began by referencing a work Dulany had penned, sharply critical of the Stamp Act,[134] praising it as a very reasoned defense of the British Constitution as the citizenry commonly understood it. Where Dulany had begun to go wrong, in Carroll's estimation, was his abandoning the "higher law for immediate gratifications" and "old principles for party attachments"; in addition, the First Citizen believed his opponent had confused "Government with the Officers of Government," the latter more often than not corrupting the former "through their desire for power and self-interest." These were a powerful few who "corrupt the life, stability, and culture of the commonwealth."[135] Because of the fee controversy and the difficulties ensuing from it, a segment of government officialdom were allowed to assume too much power; the self-termed Independent Whigs who read First Citizen's careful and scholarly argument confessed they had "for a long time impatiently waited for a man of abilities to step forward and tell our DARLING MINISTERS the evils they have brought upon the community, and what they may dread from an *injured people,* by a repetition of *despotic measures.*"[136] On February 18, the *Maryland Gazette* published Dulany's response, largely an anti-Catholic diatribe. He underscored the fact that Carroll had been a student of the Jesuits at

[133] Examples of the former would be: Coke, Blackstone Montesquieu, and Hume, while the older writers, from the time of the Roman Empire, would be such as Horace, Cicero, and Tacitus.

[134] *Considerations on the Propriety of Imposing Taxes in the British Colonies.*

[135] Birzer, 49–50.

[136] Ibid., 50.

St. Omer, could well be a Jesuit in disguise himself, was no doubt a Jacobite or follower of the deposed Catholic monarch James II in the Glorious Revolution, and, in rather bizarre fashion, went on to accuse Carroll of wishing his father's demise so that he could come to a place of complete prominence in the Maryland colony. On March 11, the *Gazette* published Carroll's response, his second letter. He made clear to Antilon, and for that matter, to all reading this correspondence, his complete and strong filial devotion to his father, stressing particularly the wonderful paternal role Charles of Annapolis had played in his life. He went on to thank the Independent Whigs for their support, declared himself to be an open enemy of Antilon (especially since the latter had resorted to personal invective), and, in an especially brilliant way, refrained from praising the coronation of the Protestant monarchs William and Mary in 1689, though also defending the right of the British people to depose James II, the last Catholic (Stuart) monarch of England. He saw these events as representative of fluctuating political factions at a time when the British constitution had not yet reached the understanding that men of Carroll's generation had come to interpret in it. Finally, not to be outdone in personal invective, Carroll raised the possibility, ever so diplomatically, that Dulany, Antilon, might well have been the author of the fee proclamation.

On no less than St. Patrick's Day 1773, Charley's Irish father, Charles of Annapolis, wrote his son that in the aftermath of the second article, "Whisper immediately Ran there is the 1st: Citizen & that every eye was fixed on You with evident marks of Pleasure and Aprobation, that many sayed they did not know which to admire most yr Strength of Reasoning or yr Calm and Gentleman like Stile Considering Antillons Scurrilous

& abusive provocation."[137] Charles of Annapolis was soon visited by prominent political Marylanders, including Samuel Chase and Daniel of St. Thomas Jennifer, solely to praise the writing of his son and to advise that, since his reasoning had been so successfully received, he should refrain from further argumentation for its own sake. And, Jennifer, admitting that, "Your Son is a most flaming Patriot and a red hot Politician," but that if it became necessary for him to argue further, he should do so on philosophical rather than legal grounds.[138]

The *Maryland Gazette* again published on March 18, 1773, and included a statement by Dulany that he did not intend to reply to Carroll because he saw little of merit in any points he raised; he would wait, rather, for one of the allies of First Citizen to put forth arguments "worthy of attention, and entitled to an answer."[139] It seemed all was polemically peaceful for a time, and the elder Carroll offered his son some practical fatherly advice:

> I think as you do that Antilon does not intend to appear again in Print, However should He alter His

[137] Charles Carroll of Annapolis to Charles Carroll of Carrollton, March 17, 1773, cited in Ronald Hoffman, Sally D. Mason, Eleanor S. Darcy, *Dear Papa, Dear Charley: The Papers of Charles Carroll of Carrollton, 1748–1782* (Chapel Hill: University of North Carolina Press, 2001), 11, 662. Hereafter cited as Hoffman, *Papers*.

[138] Birzer, 56. Daniel of St. Thomas Jennifer (1723–1790), born in Port Tobacco, Maryland, served as financial agent for the last two proprietors of Maryland, as well as a member of the Governor's Council, the Upper House of the Maryland Legislature that also served as the colony's court of appeals and as a board of senior advisors to the governor (1773–1776). As the patriot cause emerged, he soon became aligned with its objectives. He served in the Continental Congress and as president of Maryland's first senate. Ultimately, he signed the U.S. Constitution from Maryland and died in Annapolis in 1790.

[139] *Maryland Gazette*, "March 18, 1773," cited in Birzer, 58.

> Resolution upon a fresh provocation from the Whigs, before you Answer, Will it not be proper previously to Requier Him to shew that He has not advanced Many lies, for that it will be time throwne away to answer A Man who in the Opinion of the Publick has forfeited any Claim to be believed.[140]

On April 8, however, Antilon broke his silence and defended two principles he had been stressing from the outset; without fees being set by some form of law, some sort of arbitrary power would begin to be exercised, and that would be against the spirit and workings of the English constitution. His second point attacked Carroll's support of the events leading up to the abdication of James II—supporters of the Glorious Revolution praised the administration of William and Mary; Carroll, Dulany felt, believed that "the revolution was rather an act of *violence*, than of *justice*."[141] This criticism, along with others that Antilon had raised, smacked of anti-Catholicism:

> Just in case Marylanders somehow failed to take Antilon's warning about Charles Carroll's Catholicism seriously, Clericus [Philogeralethobolus] rejoined the debate, offering a history lesson about the dangers of the Jesuits. "The banishment of the Jesuits from Portugal, their prescription in France, the almost universal detestation in which they are held, the disgrace into which their leaning has fallen, seem the certain preludes of their final extermination from the face of the earth, and that it should ever be in their power to do such signal mischief to this community as some

[140] Charles Carroll of Annapolis to Charles Carroll of Carrollton, March 25, 1773, cited in Hoffman, *Papers* 11, 666.

[141] Birzer, 59.

> are inclined to persuade themselves, I can scarce be brought to think."[142]

"Where are the Whigs," Carroll of Annapolis wrote his son, "have they dropt you? I wish they would Answer Antilons Scurrility, But I would not have You doe it by any Means, you gained great Credit by the Decency of Yr last Piece & in that Piece you sayed you should have overlooked His illiberal abuse."[143] Three days later, the elder Carroll confessed that his son would easily be able to respond to Antilon's latest attack, since it was "taken up in Abuse," especially the charge made that Carroll was a "Contemptible Writer." On the contrary, "the Prepossession is so Strong & Great in Yr favour that it is not to be removed by Scurrility."[144] On May 6, 1773, Carroll wrote his third letter, emphasizing that taxes cannot be imposed by any other than the legislature, and that good, responsible citizens must be vigilant that greedy political types do not rise to the forefront to usurp the legitimate workings of government as Marylanders properly understood them. He went on to defend his own character against Antilon's accusations, stressed what was good and bad in the Glorious Revolution, took neither a Protestant nor a Jacobite position, but approved of the political principles achieved by events in 1688. "In other words," one biographer has observed,

[142] Ibid., 60. The identity of Clericus, who had previously contributed commentary to the First Citizen-Antilon debate, seems never to have come to the surface publicly.

[143] Charles Carroll of Annapolis to Charles Carroll of Carrollton, April 13, 1773, cited in Hoffman, *Papers,* 11, 678.

[144] Charles Carroll of Annapolis to Charles Carroll of Carrollton, April 16, 1773, cited in ibid., 679.

"Charles approved of the means, if not the ends; he approved of the actions, if not necessarily the actors."[145]

Maryland colonial elections of May 1773 proved the veracity of Carroll's claims—and as thought, the anti-fee, anti-proprietary forces did very well. The results "must be Mortifying endeed to the Dulanys, their Pride & Insolence is Humbled and what is still more galling," the elder Carroll wrote to his son, "they have great reason to fear an end to their Power influence & future promotion."[146] The future Signer had, to be sure, affected great change throughout the colony. Nonetheless, Dulany published his fourth and final letter in the *Maryland Gazette* on June 3, in which he once again defended the idea of fees by official proclamation, stressed that Proprietary Governor Eden had issued a proclamation which was brilliantly thought out, particularly his position on the constitutionality, long established by precedent, of officers' legitimate collecting of fees.

Dulany concluded his letter with perhaps the strongest anti-Catholic diatribe of the correspondence; Carroll, he believed, could not possibly support English liberty and patriotism while at the same time profess Roman Catholicism. Since he was a professed papist, such a position was a direct contradiction, and any reconciliation of the two would be like "holding one candle to St. Michael and another to the dragon." At considerable length, Antilon warned his readers that First Citizen's religious principles "are suspected to have so great influence, as to make it unsafe to permit his interference, in any degree, when the interests of the established religion, or the civil government

[145] Birzer, 62.

[146] Charles Carroll of Annapolis to Charles Carroll of Carrollton, May 15, 1773, cited in Hoffman, *Papers*, 11, 681.

may be concerned."[147] Carroll, for his part, brought the correspondence to a close with his final letter of July 1. He argued that Parliament must serve as a beacon of liberty, and its decisions must be grounded in the natural law. Sadly, he confessed, parliaments have often fallen short of such lofty goals. His arguments, as in the past, were liberally filled with quotes from political writers of his generation, as well as ancient Roman sources. By using such, he concluded that the Glorious Revolution, which ousted the Catholic James II and brought William and Mary to power, unintentionally brought about a period in which Parliament let down its guard and allowed the powers of the executive to become almost paramount. Such effects were soon felt in all the mother country's colonies, the fee controversy being just one practical example.

As to his Catholicism, Carroll did not respond at such length as Dulany criticized, yet he admitted that as things now stood in Maryland, the law prevented a Catholic from voting and from holding public office. Nonetheless, he asked, did this also "preclude them from thinking and writing on matters merely of a political nature?" If Antilon answered in the affirmative, Carroll felt he "would make a most excellent inquisitor. He confessed no particular aversion to the established Church of England, believed bigotry could be discovered in all religious denominations, forgave Protestants for their anti-Catholicism, testified 'I am as averse to having a religion crammed down peoples [*sic*] throats as a proclamation … [t]hese are my political principles, in which I glory[,] principles not hastily taken up to serve a turn, but what I have always avowed since I became capable of reflection.'" He concluded

[147] *Maryland Gazette*, "June 3, 1773," cited in Birzer, 69–70.

by adding that, "*We* catholicks [*sic*], who think we were badly treated ... still remember the treatment, though our resentment hath intirely [*sic*] subsided."[148]

The debate concluded, and Charles Carroll of Carrollton had become a nationally recognized spokesman for American liberty. These letters in the *Gazette* were followed with the greatest of interest in the other colonies and frequently commented upon by public and private citizens. It would serve him well as events preceding the Revolutionary War began to unfold.

Historians believe that the period of 1760–1775 saw a transformation in the American attitude from one of acquiescence in the traditional relationship with the mother country to a demand for a new order. This was clearly demonstrated by the Boston Tea Party; there seemed to no longer be a conservative group whose influence over the citizens might have persuaded them, in this case, to make amends to the British East India Company for the loss of so much of its produce, which the patriots had thrown into the Charles River. Instead American resistance was met by the passage of the Coercive Acts, closing the Port of Boston, regulating the government of Massachusetts, protecting officials attempting to carry out their duties (such as the collection of revenue), the providing of more suitable quarters for the housing of British troops in Boston, and the defeat of a measure to repeal the Tea Act. To these Coercive Acts was added the Quebec Act which, in combination with the others, became known as the Intolerable Acts.

Under the terms of the Quebec Act, the Province of Quebec, which had been created in 1763 following the Seven

148 *Maryland Gazette*, "July 1, 1773," cited in ibid., 75. The occasion of which Carroll writes is likely a reference to the events surrounding the Glorious Revolution.

Years' War between France and England, was extended to include the French-speaking settlements in the Ohio Valley and the Illinois Country areas which, according to the terms of the Proclamation of 1763, had been left without any provision for a civil government.[149] Because of the largely Roman Catholic, French-speaking character of the Province, French civil law was retained (with some modification), as well as English criminal law. The Test Act, which Catholics in England had been required to take, was modified in favor of an oath of allegiance, and the Roman Catholic religion within the Province was recognized, along with the Church's right to continue collecting tithes from her adherents.[150] The reaction of the First Continental Congress, which had convened in Philadelphia in 1774, is, to say the least, interesting:

> Nor can we express our astonishment that a British Parliament would ever consent to establish in that country a religion that has deluged your island with blood, and dispersed impiety, bigotry, persecution, murder and rebellion through every part of the world.[151]

Such anti-Catholicism was not limited to a certain segment of Congress; the body consisted of conservative thinkers such as Joseph Galloway of Pennsylvania, moderates like James Duane and John Jay of New York, extreme radicals like Sam Adams of Massachusetts and Patrick Henry and

[149] The Royal Proclamation of 1763 was issued by King George III in October of that year. It followed directly upon the Treaty of Paris of the same year, which had officially ended the Seven Years' War and transferred French territory to Great Britain.

[150] The Test Act[s] were a series of English penal laws that served as a religious test for public office and imposed significant civil disabilities on both Roman Catholics and Nonconformists.

[151] Gurn, 59.

Richard Henry Lee of Virginia. Apparently, the opinion transcended ideological differences among the delegates.

In the end, the delegates conceded to Great Britain the right to regulate the bona fide external commerce of the colonies, referred to the mother country as a "foreign power," stated that the appointment of provincial councilors in the colonies was unconstitutional and opposed to the principle of American freedom, stated essentially the same of the Declaratory Act and all pieces of legislation passed by England since 1763, and told Great Britain that, commercially, nonimportation, nonexportation, and nonconsumption would remain in effect until a redress of grievances was forthcoming.[152]

Few who have ever studied United States history are unaware of the "shot heard round the world" of April 19, 1775—the traditional opening, as it were, of the revolutionary conflict. Less than a month later, the Second Continental Congress convened, also in Philadelphia, and Carroll's fellow Marylander Thomas Johnson proposed a motion, seconded by John Adams of Massachusetts, to appoint George Washington Commander–in–Chief of the Continental Army, now poised to take up arms. The Assembly unanimously ratified the same, and Washington was officially appointed on June 15, 1775. Even now, the colonists were not advancing strong claims for independence; rather, it was British legislation rather than sovereignty that was being opposed. Only on the Fourth of July, 1776, did the next stage finally become a reality when Congress adopted the Declaration of Independence.

Early on, Congress realized the task that lay ahead could only be accomplished by the good will—and more especially

[152] For a fuller statement of this, see: Lawrence Henry Gipson, *The Coming of the Revolution: 1763–1775* (New York: Harper & Row, 1962), 229–234.

the help—of others, and with this view in mind, the importance of Canada, America's neighbor to the north, came into sharp focus. It was an important factor in the political and military considerations of both England and her colonies, and in November 1775, American forces led by General Richard Montgomery invaded Montreal; had he not been killed seven weeks later leading an invasion of Quebec, history may have been different. Within weeks, Congress knew it had to bring order out of chaos with the American forces stationed in Canada, as well as bringing the American cause into clearer focus for the Canadian people, and with this view, they passed a resolution on February 15, 1776, appointing a commission consisting of Charles Carroll of Carrollton, Samuel Chase, and Benjamin Franklin to go to Canada. John Adams had little doubt of Carroll's qualifications for such a mission, and in an oft-quoted letter to a friend, he related that:

> I was introduced to him about Eighteen Months ago in this City and was much pleased with his Conversation. He has a Fortune as I am well informed which is computed to be worth Two hundred Thousand Pounds Sterling. He is a Native of Maryland, and his Father is still living. He had a liberal Education in France and is well acquainted with the French Nation. He speaks their Language as easily as ours; and what is perhaps of more Consequence than all the rest, he was educated in the Roman Catholic Religion and still continues to worship his Maker according to the Rites of that Church. In the Cause of American Liberty his Zeal Fortitude and Perseverance have been so conspicuous that he is said to be marked out for peculiar Vengeance by the Friends of Administration; But he continues to hazard his all, his immense Fortune, the largest in America, and his

> Life. This Gentleman's Character, if I foresee aright, will hereafter make a greater Figure in America.[153]

Some two years before this appointment, and following just days after their sentiments of anti-Catholicism in the wake of the Quebec Act, the same Continental Congress had exercised what one historian has described as "statesmanship in its crudest form"[154] when, in the interest of having the Canadians throw in their lot with the colonies, proceeded to praise their religion in the warmest terms:

> We are too well acquainted with the liberality of sentiment distinguishing your nation, to imagine that any difference of religion will prejudice you against a hearty amity with us. You know that the transcendent nature of freedom elevates those who unite in her cause, above all such low-minded infirmities. The Swiss Cantons furnish a memorable proof of this truth. Their union is composed of Roman Catholic and Protestant States, living in the utmost concord and peace with one another, and thereby enabled, ever since they bravely vindicated their freedom, to defy and defeat every tyrant that has invaded them.[155]

With this background, Congress further recommended that for this mission, Charles Carroll prevail on his cousin, Fr. John Carroll, to accompany the group. Since Canada was under British sovereignty and formed a land distinct from the colonies, nothing short of the best of relations should be attempted; although under British rule, its people were practi-

153 John Adams to James Warren, February 18, 1776, cited in Smith, 137–138.

154 Gurn, 60.

155 Cited in ibid., 60.

cally all Catholics and racially French. The religious issue had become very significant, the initial imprudent comments of Congress hopefully rectified (at least in their minds), and the presence of a Catholic priest could advance the idea that the Second Continental Congress was more open-minded on religious differences than its predecessor had been.

John Carroll, destined to become the first Archbishop of Baltimore, was born in Upper Marlboro, Maryland, in 1735, the son of Daniel and Eleanor Darnall Carroll. He was related to Charles of Carrollton by blood and marriage, as all the Carroll families were interconnected. John and Charles were cousins, but not first cousins. John had presumably studied with his cousin when both were young, at Bohemia Manor on the Eastern Shore. At the age of thirteen, he was sent to the school of the English Jesuits at St. Omer in French Flanders, as was his cousin, the future Signer. He would join the Society of Jesus as a postulant at age eighteen in 1753, studied philosophy and theology at Liege, and, after fourteen years, was ordained to the priesthood in 1761. Nearly ten years later, he took final vows as a Jesuit and taught at Liege and St. Omer. He remained in Europe until he was nearly forty, and when Pope Clement XIV suppressed the Society in 1773, Fr. Carroll made arrangements to return to Maryland. He would subsequently live on his mother's farm in Rock Creek and become an itinerant missionary, ministering to the Catholic population of Maryland and Virginia. A room in his mother's house was set aside as a chapel for Catholics to assist at Mass and receive the sacraments. While here, Fr. Carroll received notification of his selection by Congress to accompany the commissioners to Canada. He weighed heavily the possible Church-state conflict which might ensue from his appointment, and, perhaps most interesting among his collected thoughts, his belief in the ultimate futility of the mission:

> The Congress has done me the distinguished and unexpected honor of desiring me to accompany the Committee ordered to Canada and of assisting them in such matters as they shall judge useful. I should betray the confidence put in me by the Honourable Congress, and perhaps disappoint their expectations were I not to open my mind to them with the utmost sincerity, and plainly tell them how little service they can hope to derive from my assistance . . . I hope I may be allowed to add, that though I have very little regard to my personal safety amidst the present distress of my country, yet I cannot help feeling my character; and I have observed that when the ministers of religion, leave the duties of their profession to take a busy part in political matters, they generally fall into contempt, and sometimes even bring discredit to the cause in whose service they are engaged. Secondly—From all the information I have been able to collect concerning the State of Canada, it appears to me that the inhabitants of that country are no wise disposed to molest the United Colonies, or prevent their forces from taking and holding possession of the strong places in that province or to assist in any manner the British arms . . . They have not the same motives for taking up arms against England which render the resistance of the other colonies so justifiable . . . Thirdly—Though I were able to bring myself to think (which as objects now appear to me I really cannot) that the Canadians

> might lawfully take up arms and concur with [*the draft of the letter stops here*][156]

Most Canadians lived in the Province of Quebec, and of their number, some 150,000 were Catholics, while Protestants numbered a mere 360. The Carroll cousins, because of their knowledge of the French language and customs, and the many years of study each had spent in Europe, were logical choices. Their instructions from Congress were quite specific:

> You are further to declare that we hold sacred the rights of conscience and may promise to the whole people, solemnly in our name, the free and undisturbed exercise of their religion; and, to the clergy, the full, perfect and peaceable possession and enjoyment of all their estates; That the government of everything related to their religion and clergy, shall be left entirely in the hands of the good people of that province and such legislature as they shall constitute: provided, however, that all other denominations of Christians be equally entitled to hold offices and enjoy civil privileges and the free exercise of their religion and be totally exempt from the payment of any tythes or taxes for the support of any religion.[157]

There were some in Congress who felt the mission of great significance, strongly feeling the Canadians must not be persuaded in any other direction than favoritism for their neighbors to the south. "I suppose you know that Doctor Franklin, Chase, and the two Mr. Carrolls are gone to

[156] Cited in Guilday, 96–97. Originally found in Msgr. Guilday's time in the Baltimore Cathedral Archives, the manuscript would now be in possession of the Archives of the Archdiocese of Baltimore.

[157] Ibid., 97–98.

Canada," Robert Morris wrote to a colleague, "for I jump in opinion with you, that Country must be ours at all events. Should it fall into the hands of the enemy they will soon raise a Nest of Hornets on our backs that will sting us to the quick."[158] While Congress may have entertained optimism over the mission, the Catholic clergy of French Canada were quite outspoken to the parishioners in their churches that all good Catholics should resist American propaganda:

> The pastoral letters of the Bishop of Quebec, Joseph Olivier Briand, were fiery in the language of warning. These pastorals of 1775–1776 reminded the French Canadians that no people had been so severe in their persecutions of Catholicism as the Bostonians had been. Nowhere were the clergy more harshly criticized than in Massachusetts. Nowhere were such invectives and blasphemies uttered against veneration of the saints in the colonies south of the Quebec boundary line. Bishop Briand warned his people against the pretended affections of the Americans and reminded them that they need never take up arms for a freedom which they already possessed. In such a climate of opinion even the sturdiest of overtures was fated to wither.[159]

In the case of Fr. Carroll, the Bishop directed that no courtesy be shown him when he arrived; were it not for a fellow ex-Jesuit with some American sympathies, Carroll might not have been able to find a place to offer Mass.

The mission to Canada began April 2, 1776, and ended on June 11, when Charles Carroll and Samuel Chase arrived in

[158] Robert Morris to Horatio Gates, April 6, 1776, cited in Annabelle Melville, *John Carroll of Baltimore: Founder of the American Catholic Hierarchy* (New York: Charles Scribner's Sons, 1955), 47.

[159] Ibid., 46.

Philadelphia. One of the more interesting documents of preserved revolutionary sources was the extensive diary Carroll kept of the entire trip. In fact, Benjamin Franklin was first to leave in early May; swelling in his legs, among other things, caused his rather sudden decision to go home. Fr. Carroll, realizing he could be of little use to a mission that seemed doomed from the start, accompanied the old patriot home and tended to his physical needs for the entire stagecoach journey home. "I find I grow daily more feeble," Franklin confessed to the other commissioners, "and I think I could hardly have got along so far but for Mr. Carroll's friendly assistance and tender care of me."[160] Later, John Carroll was to write to Charley's father of the details of their leave-taking and to assure him his son's being "safe and well."[161]

Charles Carroll, upon his return home, seemed much more enthusiastic about being chosen by the Maryland State Convention as a delegate to the Second Continental Congress in Philadelphia in 1776; much of the bitterness over the passage of the Quebec Act had abated, and the more prejudiced members of Congress had mellowed in their attitudes on the fitness of a Roman Catholic to serve in public office. As one of his biographers observed:

> His long residence in France, his fluency in the French tongue, his Catholic religion and his understanding of the French point of view all contributed to his

[160] Carl Van Doren, *Benjamin Franklin* (New York: 1938), 543, cited in Melville, 53. Note Franklin's use of the term *Mr.* rather than *Fr.*—a lack of familiarity with Catholic etiquette, no doubt, and a title he would also employ in writing to Rome suggesting Carroll's appointment to be America's first Catholic bishop.

[161] John Carroll to Charles Carroll of Annapolis, June 2, 1776, cited in ibid.

> usefulness. Various members of Congress over a social glass in Philadelphia, had hinted pretty broadly to Mr. Carroll that if the Maryland Convention should see fit to elect him again as a delegate—and everybody knew that the First Citizen could get anything he wanted out of that same Maryland Convention—Congress would welcome him with considerable enthusiasm.[162]

For more than two years, Carroll had studied the legal, constitutional, historical, and contemporary arguments regarding the colonies' relations with England; he had forcefully argued for colonial sovereignty, and now that George III had taken the actions he did, Carroll had no choice but to argue, from a legal perspective, for the cause of American independence. In fact, such arguments were rooted in natural rights and the law of nature:

> As Suarez had said, political authority derives from the people in the divine process of nature as it affects life in society. Locke had further clarified the origin of the authority finally transferred into a governmental form. In terms of a *compact* with the people, a ruler must exercise that authority. Carroll had insisted that authority had originated in the province of Maryland and her sister colonies. The Maryland Charter was itself a compact of people and ruler—spelled out with particulars of the people's rights to their own parliament and other freedoms. Now at last the charter was officially rejected by the King.[163]

[162] Smith, 156. Smith observes that "there is every reason to believe that he was asked to be a Delegate to the [First Continental] Congress [and] he refused." Ibid., 120.

[163] Thomas O'Brien Hanley, S.J., *Revolutionary Statesman: Charles Carroll and the War* (Chicago: Loyola University Press, 1983), 152. Hereafter cited as Hanley, *War.*

Carroll's contributions were by now well recognized, and he was easily chosen as a delegate to the Second Continental Congress from Maryland, along with Matthew Tilghman, Thomas Johnson Jr., William Paca, Samuel Chase, Thomas Stone, and Robert Alexander. On July 1, 1776, the unanimous declaration of the Maryland Convention favoring independence was placed before Congress. Carroll officially took his seat in the Second Continental Congress on July 18, the first time a Catholic had ever occupied such a position on the national level. On August 2, Carroll officially affixed his signature to the Declaration of Independence, in company with many of his fellow delegates.

> A remarkable story is still told concerning an incident which is said to have taken place when Carroll affixed his signature to our Charter of liberty ... When it came time for the Marylanders to sign, John Hancock, President of Congress, inquired of Carroll whether he was willing to subscribe. Carroll replied that he would sign with pleasure. Then he advanced and wrote "Charles Carroll" on the parchment. The delegates now began jocular discussion as to whether, should the Revolution fail, they would hang singly or hang together. One remarked to Carroll that he would readily escape the royal vengeance, on account of there being so many Charles Carrolls. Whereupon Carroll again took the pen and added the words 'of Carrollton' to the name he had already written, to facilitate his identification in the event of his being required to answer for his treason.[164]

[164] Gurn, 83–84. The author adds a eulogy delivered on Carroll decades later by Chauncey M. Depew, the well-known capitalist and orator, on the greatness of Carroll's action that day. One half-century later, in 1826, Carroll received two facsimile copies of the original Declaration of Independence, engrossed on parchment,

Despite the advancement he had made up to this point on the national scene, there were some among his friends, in England and the new nation, who believed the Roman Catholic Church to be one of a number of ways one could work out one's salvation—such being the case, and considering the position of Catholics at this point in the eighteenth century, Carroll was advised he might want to explore another means—a church far more acceptable to the emerging American mind. No doubt his father, Charles of Annapolis, would have exploded at such a suggestion, but his son seemed to take a more reasoned approach in writing to one of his British friends, expressing the view that his Catholicism should not hinder him in his advancement:

> Well I see you want to make a convert of me, not out of religious zeal. But all modes of Religion being in yr estimation indifferent to our Creator, I may as well embrace that which my countrymen have embraced …

with an enclosed letter noting that, "Of this document, unparalleled in the annals of mankind, the original, deposited in this department, exhibits your name as one of the subscribers. The rolls herewith transmitted are copies as exact as the art of engraving can present, of the instrument itself, as well as of the Signers to it. While performing the duty thus assigned me, permit me to felicitate you, and the country which is reaping the rewards of your labors as well; that your hand was affixed to this record of glory, as that, after the lapse of nearly half a century, you survive to receive this tribute of reverence and gratitude from your children, the present fathers of the land. With every sentiment of veneration, I have the honor of subscribing myself your fellow citizen. JOHN QUINCY ADAMS." The documents were presented at Doughoregan Manor, September 15, 1826. John Quincy Adams served as sixth President of the United States from 1825–1829. He was the son of the revolutionary patriot John Adams, who served as the nation's second president. Leonard, 132–133.

> What if they have embraced an absurd one? Yes, certainly, because ye one I have been brought up in is still more absurd. Granted, for argument's sake; What, then, do you advise me to quit a false religion & adopt one equally false, and this merely to humour the prejudices of fools, or to be on a footing with knaves? I have too much sincerity and too much pride to do either, even if my filial love did not restrain me—for I can truly say, *Nequeo lachrymas perferre parentis.* I am a warm friend to toleration; I execrate ye intolerating spirit of ye Church of Rome, and of other Churches, for she is not singular in that. Designing & selfish men invented religious tests to exclude from posts of profit & trust their weaker or more conscientious fellow-subjects, thus to secure for themselves all ye emoluments of Government.[165]

Throughout the war years, Charles Carroll's role was one of a statesman rather than a military combatant. His correspondence throughout the conflict with the mother country are filled with sentiments favorable to the patriot cause, and to it he gave his all. Two episodes in particular show his determination in the cause of freedom—the controversy over the Conway Cabal, as well as the *Peggy Stewart* affair. The former was an ill-fated attempt to remove George Washington, Carroll's good friend, from his position as commander of the American forces.

From the time of his appointment by John Adams in 1775, there had been a faction opposed to him; John Hancock, from the same state of Massachusetts, felt quite certain he was to be appointed. Not only a state kinship, Hancock felt, but he undoubtedly was part of the solid

[165] Charles Carroll of Carrollton to William Graves, August 15, 1774 (*Maryland Historical Magazine*, xxxii, 222–3, cited in Smith, 122).

Massachusetts front against the perceived pretentions of Virginia. Up to now, the war had been essentially a New England one, and Adams knew well (as did others) that placing a New Englander as Commander–in–Chief could be a fatal mistake. Hancock very gracefully bowed out, coming quickly to the conclusion that as the war progressed, if the Virginian Washington did not measure up, someone more acceptable might be chosen. The two most interested contenders for Washington's position, to be sure, were Major General Charles Lee and Brigadier General Horatio Gates, either of whom would have been acceptable to the anti-Washington faction in Congress.

There were a fair number in Congress who felt Washington had been a poor choice for commander, though Congress as a whole knew little of the workings of practical warfare—the experienced fighting men in America were in uniform, but Congress, feeling itself superior to any military organization, felt it should call the shots. In fact, Washington had suffered a number of significant losses during the first two years of the war. After his defeats at Brandywine and Germantown, Horatio Gates seemed to turn the whole course of the war by defeating British General Burgoyne at Saratoga—a feather in his cap and anything but good news for Washington. Many of the General's friends in Congress began to worry about his future and perhaps became more worried with Washington's response, one of choosing to ignore the entire thing and carry on with the full plentitude of power Congress had bestowed on him.

"Unless he does," Charles Carroll wrote his father, "our affairs will never go well; but he is so humane & delicate that I fear the common cause will suffer from his humanity & delicacy of temper: however I believe he is determined to act with more vigor than heretofore: this man cannot be too much admired."[166] The opposition to the Virginian had managed to reorganize the Board of War in November 1777 and placed Horatio Gates as president—a slap to Washington in placing Gates in a position of superiority. What constituted a positive note for the Commander were the appointments of both Charles Carroll and Gouverneur Morris of Pennsylvania, two of Washington's staunchest supporters, to the same Board. Both men were extremely formidable, and rather easily moved the Board of War to their side.

> It is unlikely that Gates ever had a real chance to win Washington's post. No one ventured to propose on the floor of Congress that Washington be removed. General Thomas Conway, Irish-born French officer who had joined the Continentals said or hinted in a letter to Gates that he hoped Gates would supersede Washington. The fact was revealed apparently by James Wilkinson, Gates' aid, while drunk. The subsequent behavior of Conway, Gates and Wilkinson exposed them to ridicule from Washington's supporters, and it became patent hat a drive to dismiss the commander in chief would surely fail.[167]

Conway was later challenged to a duel, seriously injured, and, believing himself at death's door, wrote a sincerely apologetic letter to Washington. He later served with distinction in the French army.

[166] Charles Carroll of Carrollton to Charles Carroll of Annapolis, September 23, 1777, cited in Smith, 175.

[167] John Richard Alden, *The American Revolution* (New York: Harper & Row, 1954), 199.

The *Peggy Stewart* affair, more localized at Annapolis, Maryland, was also an event that involved Charles Carroll during the war period. In October 1774, this brig had arrived in the Port of Annapolis, carrying about fifty indentured servants and more than a ton of English tea. This is, of course, after the Continental Congress has passed articles of nonimportation, nonexportation, and nonconsumption of any and all English goods. The brig's owner was Anthony Stewart, and he was carrying the tea into port for James and Joseph Williams, local merchants, who later claimed they had ordered the tea before nonimportation had taken effect. Stewart himself was a much-respected citizen of Annapolis and a close friend of Charles Carroll, the two both members of the socially prestigious Hominy Club. At a public hearing of irate citizens, the captain of the brig went so far as to say he had not realized there was tea on board—a comment that sent the crowd into uproarious laughter. A majority of citizens would have been content to let Mr. Stewart off with the confiscation of his tea and having him read aloud a public apology he had written; a vociferous minority called for tarring and feathering as the least punishment. A long-standing tradition held that at some point Stewart consulted with his friend Carroll—what transpired has never come to light, but Stewart on his own initiative, burned the brig, applying a torch in the presence of a large and enthusiastic crowd. "If the painting in the Maryland State House is true history," one Carroll biographer has written, "Mr. Stewart carried off his humiliation with an air which won him considerable respect."[168]

[168] Smith, 127. Indentured servants were those who secured their passage to the new world by "indenturing" themselves to a particular individual or family, agreeing to work seven years in return before they secured their freedom. They are often called "His Majesty's Seven-Year Passengers."

In August, 1776, after signing the Declaration of Independence, Carroll's next concern, and one which occupied much of his political thought, was the formation of his state's new constitution. Among those considered kindred spirits were the planters, merchants, and Catholics. Approximately one-twelfth of Maryland's population were Catholic, and nearly all of those supported the revolutionary effort. Opposition to these groups was found in the artisans and mechanics, in both Annapolis and Baltimore; the latter was rapidly increasing in population and provided an ongoing source of democratic agitation.

It appears shortly after signing the Declaration of Independence that Carroll had some misgivings; a break from the mother country could spell the onslaught of internal divisions in the new governments formed on both the state and national levels; such divisions could well end up in the formation of despotic governments with their respective leaders, and since reunion with Britain was now unlikely, other solutions must be found to prevent such governmental chaos. One thing was surely required, namely, leadership groups must make "meaningful concessions to the popular spirit, which the rhetoric and dislocation of the times had inflamed. With the traditional underpinnings of political authority—class prerogative and rightful privilege—swept away, the newer assertive 'meaner sort' demanded recognition and the accommodation of formerly ignored needs."[169]

Carroll began by appealing to the gentlemen of Maryland to "assert themselves," because if they did not mobilize, "this Province will in a short time be involved in all the horrors of an ungovernable & revengeful Democracy, &

[169] Hoffman and Mason II, 858.

will be dyed with the blood of its best citizens." He went on to claim that if the elite asserted themselves forcefully enough, "we shall be able to establish a very good government in this State,"[170] better, one would think, than any other type devised in any of the former colonies.

Apparently, Carroll exerted much influence on the thinking and practical results that emerged from the new document, especially its Declaration of Rights. Based on the social compact theory, the Constitution called for mixed government, appealed to popular sovereignty, but came down quite emphatically against the dominance of the popular will. Its first article reiterates that "government of right originates from the people, is found in compact only, and instituted solely for the good of the whole."[171] The three branches of state government were to be separate and distinct from each other, judges were given life tenures, but the state assembly was favored in that any "power of suspending laws, or the execution of laws, unless by or derived from the legislature"[172] was forbidden. The public liberty was safeguarded from any sort of despotism by the composition of the upper house of the legislature—the Senate—by insuring the "disinterestedness and excellence of the fifteen senators:"[173] each had to own at least one thousand pounds in American currency, and they were chosen by an electoral college comprised of two delegates from each Maryland county; each of these individuals had to own at least five hundred pounds American currency. Finally, the executive was denied the power of the veto, and the concept of judicial review

[170] Charles Carroll of Carrollton to Charles Carroll of Annapolis, August 20, 1776, cited in McDermott, 149.

[171] Cited in ibid., 149.

[172] Ibid., 150.

[173] Ibid.

was eliminated.[174] The state also extended religious freedom to all Christians; the Declaration of Rights restricted office holding in the state to Christians by means of an oath.

As the war for independence progressed, Charles Carroll became as concerned as many of his fellow citizens as to its outcome, and the many problems which likely would ensue before victory could be won. He expressed some of those concerns to his friend Benjamin Franklin:

> I flatter myself our struggles for Independence will, in the end, be crowned with success, but we must suffer much in the meantime, and unless we continue to receive powerful assistance in arms, ammunition, and clothing, and other warlike stores, and supplies of cash or a credit in Europe, equivalent thereto, we must sink under the efforts of a rich and inveterate enemy, mistress of the ocean, and determined, it seems, to run every hazard in subduing these States to unconditional submission. My greatest apprehensions arise from the depreciation of our paper money; if we emit more bills of credit they will fall to nothing; we cannot tax to the amount of the charges of the war, and of our civil establishments; we must then raise money by lotteries or by borrowing."

Interestingly, he adds this postscript:

> If this war should be of any considerable duration, we shall want men to recruit our armies; could we engage five or six thousand men, German, Swiss, or the Irish brigade? I have mentioned this matter to several members of Congress, but they did not seem to relish the

[174] Judicial review has traditionally been defined as the power given to the courts (federal or state) to review executive or legislative actions in conformity with the fundamental law of the sovereignty involved.

> introduction of foreign mercenaries. I own it ought to be avoided if possible.[175]

Charles Carroll was, in fact, not the first of his countrymen to entertain such fears and to realize the importance of foreign aid. Many of the leaders of the new nation knew that a decisive military victory over the mother country was not something that could be achieved by American efforts alone. Months before the formal declaration of independence in 1776, Congress had set up a secret committee to make friendly overtures to potential European friends. Silas Deane of Connecticut was sent to Paris, ostensibly as a merchant seeking out supplies and credit. He quickly discovered that simply because we were England's revolting colonies, and England was the centuries-old enemy of France, aid to the war effort was something the French government was favorably disposed to. In fact, since the close of the Seven Years' War in 1763,[176] France had been looking for an opportunity to weaken its archenemy, and the chance now seemed to be presenting itself. A French playwright, and sometime amateur diplomat, Caron de Beaumarchais had been in contact with another American agent in London, Arthur Lee, and these three were joined by the French Foreign Minister Comte de Vergennes in persuading the monarch, Louis XVI, that aid to the American colonies was in France's best interests.[177]

[175] Charles Carroll of Carrollton to Benjamin Franklin, August 12, 1777, in Rowland, i, 207, 209.

[176] Also often referred to as the French and Indian War.

[177] The French government was able to persuade Spain to join the cause; by the standard of those days, France contributed nearly two million dollars in subsidies and nearly six and one half million dollars in loans; Spain, approximately four hundred thousand in subsidies and two hundred fifty thousand in loans.

After the Declaration of Independence had been signed and proclaimed worldwide, the government sent Benjamin Franklin to Paris to join those there and to secure from the French recognition of the United States as an independent nation. Though fully in sympathy with American war aims, Vergennes was reluctant to offer full diplomatic recognition to the United States, thus risking war with England; should an event occur which proved positive the winning of independence, the French government would likely do an about-face.

> Such evidence was not forthcoming until December, 1777, when news arrived that General Burgoyne's British army, thrusting down from Montreal into New York, had been forced to surrender, to General [Horatio] Gates at Saratoga. This was what Vergennes had been waiting for; he tried to enlist Spain in the cause and when Spain procrastinated, resolved that France would proceed without her. On December 17 the American commissioners were informed that France would grant recognition and make a treaty with the United States, and on February 6, 1778, a treaty of amity and commerce and a treaty of alliance were signed in Paris, the latter to take effect if Great Britain went to war with France because of the former. Vergennes had hastened to take this action because of fear that if he did not, England would effect a reconciliation with her former colonies. Burgoyne's surrender had produced a sensation in England and led the ministry to offer liberal terms of settlement to the Americans. In March, Parliament passed a series of bills repealing

> all the legislation enacted since 1763 of which the colonists had complained.[178]

News arrived in the new nation that the Treaty of Paris, officially ending the War for American Independence, had been signed on April 19, 1782, just eight years from the date of the Battle of Lexington when the "shot heard round the world" had begun hostilities. One of Charles Carroll's biographers notes that the great patriot of Doughoregan Manor never tired of citing the contribution of his coreligionists to the cause of independence:

> In connection with the close of the war it has been sometimes recalled but not often if ever printed that nearly if not quite 70 percent of the men who won the battle of Yorktown for our cause and practically ended the war with Great Britain were men professing the Roman Catholic religion. At first glance you wonder how this could be[,] knowing that the Catholics of the time formed but a small per cent of the population. But you will recall that the army of Count Rochambeau of about 8,000 and the men in DeGrasse fleet some 2,000 were Catholic while Washington's army numbered some 10,000 of whom many were Irish, French and Colonial Catholics. So it is well within bounds to say

[178] Julius W. Pratt, *A History of United States Foreign Policy* (Englewood Cliffs, New Jersey: Prentice-Hall, 1955), 20. Pratt contends that the treaty with France constituted the only "entangling alliance" in which the United States participated until the middle of the twentieth century. Such alliances, George Washington noted carefully in his Farewell Address to the nation, were to be avoided at all costs. In the winning of independence, however, it is Pratt's thesis that such an approach as the Treaty of Amity and Commerce took was indispensable.

> that 70 per cent of the force that captured Cornwallis was made up of Catholics.[179]

Carroll, for his part, was preeminent in Maryland life and would soon find himself in the United States Senate. Through the years, he had kept up two mansions, one at Doughoregan and the other at Spa Creek in the harbor of Annapolis. The victory celebration following the declaration of American Independence was celebrated at Maryland's capital:

> "There is to be a grand dinner on Squire Carroll's point," wrote Mrs. Walter Dulany, "a whole ox is to be roasted & I can't tell how many sheep and calves ... liquor in proportion." Fireworks and a ball followed the banquet.[180]

Just one month after this celebration, George Washington came to Annapolis, where the Congress was then sitting, to resign his commission. From this point, it appeared Washington would devote his efforts to strengthen the federal government. He was the finest choice to be selected the nation's first chief executive within a few years, as well as the newly formed Federalist Party's most convincing spokesman.

> The resignation took place in the small Senate chamber in the state house. A throng of visitors crowded around the Senators' fifteen desks as Washington, clad in his buff and blue uniform, surrendered power to the nation's representatives. Carroll was there on the floor with his daughters. Martha Washington and her two Custis grandchildren sat in the gallery overhead. John

[179] Leonard, 201.
[180] McDermott, 190.

> Trumbull's rendering of the scene adorns the United States Capital Rotunda.[181]

The new nation was now beginning; the career of America's first Catholic statesman would continue for another half-century.

[181] Ibid.

CHAPTER 4

MR. CARROLL: CATHOLIC AND STATESMAN

Part 1: Catholic

To say Charles Carroll of Carrollton was a devout, actively practicing Catholic is a long-established historical fact; to say that as a Catholic and a statesman he was one in whom his coreligionists could take great pride is also well verified. His day began in the earliest morning hours with at least prayers in chapel, or, when a priest was resident at Doughoregan, the Holy Sacrifice of the Mass. He was vitally concerned throughout his life that his family's Catholic heritage remain intact—not the easiest of tasks given the frequency of mixed marriages in colonial and revolutionary society. His library contained the finest of Catholic volumes, both from his student days in France and those he had accumulated over the years. His cousin Fr. John Carroll was quickly rising to prominence in his native land after an equally if not superior education to that of Charles in Europe, and he would go on to become the nation's first Catholic bishop.

The Carrolls, Charles in particular, were the inheritors of deep-seated hostility to their religious creed. "A universal anti-

Catholic bias was brought to Jamestown in 1607," Msgr. John Tracy Ellis observed, "and vigilantly cultivated in all thirteen colonies from Massachusetts to Georgia."[182] This bias "emerged in Maryland even in the time of Leonard and Cecil Calvert and had its source in the bigotry both encroaching from neighboring Virginia and welling up within Maryland itself where, from the beginning, Protestants were always the majority."[183]

Charles Carroll saw a bit of this directed to himself shortly before he was commissioned by Congress to go to Canada. Many in Congress were angered to have any Catholic representing them and, at very least, hoped Carroll's Catholicism could be played down; John Adams, for example, wrote to a friend prior to the mission that, "Your prudence will direct you to communicate the circumstances of the Priest, the Jesuit, and the *Romish* religion, only to such persons as can judge of the measure upon large and generous principles, and will not indiscreetly divulge it."[184] About the same time, the chaplain of the Continental Congress, one Jacob Duché, lamented to George Washington that, "Maryland no longer sends a Tilghman and a Protestant Carroll."[185] Still more excitable was a broadside written by Benedict Arnold, issued after his treason, urging others to do what he had done.

> What security remains to you even for the enjoyment of the consolations of that religion for which your fathers braved the ocean, the heathen, and the

[182] John Tracy Ellis, *American Catholicism* (Chicago: University of Chicago Press, 1956), 19.

[183] Van Devanter, 83–84.

[184] John Adams to James Warren, February 18, 1776, cited in Smith, 203.

[185] Gurn, 133. Charles Carroll the Barrister, a cousin of the Signer, was of a Protestant line of the Carrolls.

> wilderness? Do you know that the eye which guides this pen, lately saw your mean and profligate Congress at Mass for the soul of a Roman Catholic in purgatory, and participating in the rites of a church, against whose antichristian corruptions your pious ancestors would have witnessed with their blood?[186]

Carroll was, of course, poignantly aware of such events and mindsets, and, at an outdoor Mass at Doughoregan Manor in 1937, commemorating the two hundredth anniversary of the Signer's birth, noted Church historian Msgr. Peter Guilday reminded a congregation in excess of thirty thousand:

> It must be realized that, in spite of his wealth, education, and culture, in spite of the social standing of which the anti-Catholic laws of Maryland could not rob him, Charles Carroll of Carrollton, as he was henceforth known, returned a disfranchised citizen, with no voice in the political affairs of the province. As a Catholic, he was only a little better politically than the slaves on the plantation. He was denied the public exercise of his religion, and was forced by these same laws to pay a double tax for the support of a clergy that could never be his own. Events, however, of far reaching importance were soon to brush aside this civic injustice; and before he realized it, he was in the thick of the political controversies of the day.[187]

[186] *Rivington's Gazette,* November 1, 1780, cited in Smith, 204. The agent of the Spanish government had died while visiting Washington's camp at Morristown, New Jersey, and some American dignitaries attended his funeral Mass at Old St. Mary's, Philadelphia.

[187] John H. Scarff (ed.), *The Bicentenary Celebration of the Birth of Charles Carroll of Carrollton: 1737–1937* (Baltimore: The Lord Baltimore Press, 1937), 23.

This notwithstanding, Carroll's Catholic Faith had so deeply taken root that the particulars surrounding life in early America were not the serious impediments one might think. As one commentator has put it:

> The Catholic community in Maryland endorsed, contributed to, fought for, and died for an ideology that rested upon republican principles and came wrapped in the rhetoric of anti-Catholicism. On the surface, it was an almost absurd incongruence—one that the British essayist Samuel Johnson seized upon in 1776, when he noted with great sarcasm that all of Maryland's residents "are now become such excellent Protestants," that they "totally forget that their own existence as a Colony is owing to this very religion which [the Sons of Liberty] abhor."[188]

It was in this atmosphere that the Carroll family lived and religiously prospered. The tradition of which the family was a part had roots in the seventeenth century, both in England and Maryland.

For generations, the Catholic laity were nourished by English Jesuits in the traditional ideas found in the *Spiritual Exercises of St. Ignatius of Loyola*. Maryland Catholic libraries in the great manor homes attest to this, as to devotion to the Sacred Heart of Jesus, also deeply rooted in Jesuit tradition. The writings of St. Francis de Sales also impacted on Catholic Marylanders, especially in practical ways to sanctify their daily lives.

> It is more difficult to estimate the way in which religious culture among Catholic Marylanders was affected by the

[188] Maura Jane Farrelly, *Papist Patriots: The Making of an American Catholic Identity* (Oxford University Press, 2012), 122, cited in Connor, 144.

> recollection of English Catholic martyrs. The religious combat theme in Robert Persons, SJ, who lived as a hunted priest in the late Elizabethan and early James I eras, must have had some influence in America, judging from the libraries that held his volumes. His *Directorium* was a guide to the spiritual life as seen by one who had also written treatises showing the illegitimacy of Elizabeth's claim to the throne of England. Charles Carroll of Carrolton's father, who had such books in his library, indeed reflected the militancy of Persons ... Maryland Catholics certainly possessed a spirituality which left them inclined to fight for the freedom of their Faith. The English Catholic gentry, it would seem, were quite different in this respect. Richard Challoner's book, *Garden of the Soul*, did not carry a militant message, and some commentators note that the title symbolizes a siege mentality and social withdrawal. Maryland conditions were not as harsh and Catholics had greater hopes of emancipation in America. They moved with considerable spirit, intent upon improving their religious lot. They showed a greater sense of responsibility and leadership in the role which they held as gentlemen.[189]

Charles Carroll made certain his family had the finest of European Catholic educations, much as he and generations before him had. Of the three who survived to adulthood, his daughters were Mary and Catharine; the former married

[189] Thomas O'Brien Hanley, S.J., *The American Revolution and Religion: Maryland: 1770–1800* (Washington, DC: The Catholic University of America Press, 1971), 176. Hereafter cited as Hanley, *American Revolution*. Bishop Richard Challoner (the title of Bishop was prohibited for Catholic prelates in England in the eighteenth century) was Vicar Apostolic of the London District and, as such, the religious superior of the clergy in America after the suppression of the Society of Jesus.

Richard Caton, and the latter, Robert Goodloe Harper. His son, Charles of Homewood, married Harriet Chew of Philadelphia, daughter of Benjamin Chew, a Quaker-born legal scholar who eventually became Chief Justice of the Supreme Court of Pennsylvania.[190]

Richard Caton was a native Englishman from Lancashire in the north. From all accounts, Mary's father was aghast: she had not previously announced any sort of engagement to Caton, something which was not done in the eighteenth century, and to a young man of whom the family knew nothing. The Signer expressed his displeasure in a letter to a cousin:

> My daughter, I am sorry to inform you is much attached to, and has engaged herself to a young English gentleman of the name of Caton. I do sincerely wish she had placed her affections elsewhere, but I do not think myself at liberty to control her choice, when fixed on a person of unexceptionable character, nor would you, I am sure, desire that I should. My assent to this union is obtained on these two conditions, that the young gentleman shall extricate himself from some debts which he has contracted, and shall get into a business sufficient to maintain himself and a family. These conditions he has promised to comply with, and when performed there will be no other impediment in the way of his marriage.[191]

[190] In later years, Chew left the Quakers and became a member of the Church of England.

[191] Charles Carroll of Carrollton to Daniel Carroll of Duddington, March 13, 1787, in Rowland, 11, 104. Daniel Carroll of Duddington was the eldest son of Charles Carroll of Duddington, the grandson of Daniel Carroll of Duddington. He had accompanied his cousin Charles Carroll of Homewood (the Signer's son) to the English Jesuit College at Liege and had apparently strongly desired to become a suitor to his cousin Mary Carroll. It would appear the

Carroll's daughter Catharine was to marry Robert Goodloe Harper of South Carolina, a non-Catholic who would relocate and become a significant force in the Federalist Party in Maryland in the early Republic. A native Virginian, Harper had studied law in Charleston, eventually entered politics, and was elected to the South Carolina House of Representatives and then to Congress to fill a vacancy caused by the death of a member from South Carolina. He eventually moved to Baltimore where he also practiced law. Catharine (Kitty) Carroll met him when she was twenty-two, and, though he had great charm, he also had great debts, and once again,

---

Signer was writing the young man as a courtesy, informing him of his daughter's choice. Caton, for his part, apparently attained the good graces of his father-in-law, as is recorded by another chronicler of the family: "After her marriage Mrs. Caton, the daughter of Charles Carroll of Carrollton, lived at Brooklandwood. Her husband, Richard Caton, also owned Catonsville, a country-seat, whose suburbs and ancient village are called after him," Field, 181. The Catons were the parents of four daughters, of whom, three settled in Europe and were called "The American Graces" because of their high social standing. Marianne, married first to Robert Patterson of Baltimore (whose sister Elizabeth had married Jerome Bonaparte, brother of Napoleon), and after his death, married Richard, Marquess Wellesley (brother of the Duke of Wellington), Lord Lieutenant of Ireland, and figured prominently as a Catholic among Protestant Anglo-Irish. Louisa became the Dutchess of Leeds, and a member of Queen Victoria's Court, Elizabeth married George Jerningham, Lord Staford, and made a fortune speculating in the stock market. Only one sister, Emily, remained in Maryland; married to a native Scottish, Canadian businessman, John MacTavish, she managed the family's vast holdings, and, through her closeness with the Redemptorist Fathers, persuaded her sisters to transfer their Annapolis property to their congregation. The most complete work to date on the Graces is: Jehanne Wake, *Sisters of Fortune: America's Caton Sisters at Home and Abroad* (New York: Simon & Schuster, 2010).

Charles Carroll was faced with the very real possibility of a fortune hunter, interested solely in his daughter's fortune. For a lengthy time, he was not allowed to call on Kitty at Doughoregan, but Carroll finally relented, largely due to the intervention of Richard Caton, who seemed to convince his father-in-law that Harper could just as easily establish financial stability as he apparently had done. In addition, Harper was a Protestant, albeit a lukewarm one. Though Carroll seems not to have raised religion as his major objection, he did foresee difficulties in the raising of the children. Nonetheless, he finally consented to his daughter's plans, and the couple was married in Annapolis by Archbishop Carroll, the Signer's cousin, in 1801. Their children were indeed raised in the Catholic Faith and sent to parochial boarding schools; the Harpers, for their part, seemed to manage quite well:

> Oakland, the estate Harper eventually constructed, on the Falls Road in northern Baltimore, became a social mecca at which the Harpers entertained grandly and lavishly. One guest recorded in his diary that at one affair the guests arrived for over two hours and then danced and promenaded under the shadows of the huge trees surrounding the estate, pausing only to refresh themselves with strawberries and cream, cherries and ices of all sorts.[192]

The marriage of Charles Carroll's son, Charles of Homewood, was an initial cause of concern, again for religious reasons.

[192] Joseph W. Fox, *Champion of Southern Federalism: Robert Goodloe Harper of South Carolina* (Port Washington, NY: Kennikat Press, 1972), 213. Harper later became recognized as a skilled debater, had an excellent command of the law, and practiced before the Supreme Court. His marriage connections naturally attracted prestigious clients to his law firm.

The Chew family of Philadelphia were staunch Episcopalians and insisted the marriage be performed in that sect, with the Episcopal Bishop William White presiding. In fact, Charles of Homewood had invited Archbishop Carroll to come to the city to officiate at the wedding, and his cousin had accepted. Upon arriving, and discovering a far more elaborate ceremony had been planned with the Protestant clergyman presiding, the Archbishop would have no part of a compromise and wrote to his cousin the Signer stating that:

> I resolved immediately not to enter into this compromise. Neither I nor any other Catholic clergyman can perform the ceremony under present circumstances. Mrs. Caton and her sister are determined not to be present at the marriage if performed by any but a Catholic minister. If Charles should finally acquiesce in the proposal to be married by Bishop White, your daughter will not be present at the nuptials but return with me.[193]

[193] Archbishop John Carroll to Charles Carroll of Carrolton, July 15, 1800, cited in Gurn, 184. Curiously, an early account of this event by Esmeralda Boyle in her *Biographical Sketches of Distinguished Marylanders* has Archbishop Carroll and his niece arriving together, and after a brief conversation, Charles of Homewood decided in favor of the Faith of his family to have his cousin officiate according to the rite of the Catholic Church, after which Protestant Bishop White conducted an Episcopal wedding service. Whichever account prevails, the outcome was successful; the Catholic wedding occurred in Old St. Joseph's Church on Willings Alley with Archbishop Carroll officiating. For his part, Charles Carroll of Homewood turned out a great disappointment to his father, who outlived him by some years. He was an excessive drinker, which surely shortened his life. It was rumored he had been much in love with Nellie Custis, the granddaughter of Martha Washington. Washington had attended the wedding of Sophia Chew to John Eager Howard, but it is not certain whether he attended Harriet's to Carroll.

With matters resolved, Charles Carroll showed a strong side to his Catholic Faith in writing to his daughter-in-law:

> I am much gratified by your assurances that your daughters shall be brought up in the R[oman] C[atholic] religion; it is my wish and their father's also that they should be; unfortunately, though at present he has little religion himself, he is quite in earnest that his daughters should be religious; he as many others under the influence of passions know and feel the importance of religion though they do not live up to its precepts. Being persuaded that there can be but one true religion taught by Christ, and that the R[oman] C[atholic] is that religion, I conceive it to be my duty to have my grandchildren brought up in it. I feel no ill will or illiberal prejudices against the sectarians which have abandon[ed] that faith; if their lives be conformable to the duties and morals prescribed by the Gospel, I have the charity to hope and believe they will be rewarded with eternal happiness, though they may entertain erroneous doctrines in point of faith; the great number in every religion not having the leisure or means to investigate the truth of the doctrines they have been taught, must rest their religious faith on their instructors, and therefore the great body of the people may conscientiously believe that they hold the true faith; but they who, from liberal education, from understanding, from books, not written by one party only, and from leisure, have the means of examining into the truth of the doctrines they have been taught as orthodox, are in my opinion bound to make the examination, nor suffer early instructions or impressions or habits or prejudices

---

The Carrolls became the parents of seven children, including John Lee Carroll, a future Governor of Maryland.

> to operate against the conviction of what is right. Upon conviction only a change of religion is desirable; on a concern so seriously interesting to all of us no worldly motives should sway our conduct.[194]

Years earlier, he sent a missive to his daughter Mary, proving him convincingly knowledgeable about matters of faith, as they found their way into theological controversy. A gentleman had called on Carroll at Doughoregan, who told him he knew his daughter:

> He is a quaker and has read Thomas a Kempis, Fenelon and Massillon's sermons. By his account the quakers, or at least many of them, read Roman Catholick books; few, if any of that sect embrace our religion, I believe. Grahame alluded to the writings of Fenelon about the love of God; you have read or heard of the celebrated dispute on that subject between Fenelon and Bossuet; the writings, or rather the opinions of the former were condemned by the Pope; they were judged to be too mystical and rapturous. The pure love of God, my dear Mary, remained with the frailties of our nature (the piety, great learning and excellent understanding of Fenelon did not prevent him from running into error on this subject) can alone make us happy in this life and nothing else can secure our happiness in the next.[195]

[194] Charles Carroll of Carrollton to Harriet Carroll, August 29, 1816, cited in Gurn, 191.

[195] Charles Carroll of Carrollton to Mary Carroll Caton, March 5, 1793, cited in Field, 169. François Fénelon (1651–1715) was a French Catholic archbishop, theologian, poet, and writer. Jacques-Bénigne Bossuet (1627–1704) was a French bishop, pulpit orator with a masterful style, and theologian.

Charles Carroll's Catholic life also saw the parallel development of the career of his cousin, Fr. John Carroll, destined to become the country's first bishop upon the creation of the See of Baltimore in 1789, the same year the new Federal Constitution became operative. At the time of its erection, the Diocese of Baltimore encompassed the territory from the border of Canada to the border of Florida and from the east coast to the Mississippi River. It would remain such until 1808, with its erection as an archdiocese, and the creation of the Suffragan Sees of New York, Philadelphia, Boston, and Bardstown, Kentucky.[196]

John Carroll's episcopal career likely began later than necessary; there was a feeling rampant in this country, as well as in England, that the presence of a bishop would be viewed as contrary to the prevailing concept of separation of church and state. Such seemed to be the case for the Protestant Episcopal Church in the United States as well. *Propaganda Fide* in Rome, unfamiliar with American ways, sought opinion; Benjamin Franklin, as good example, feared an English prelate might be detrimental politically, and that, perhaps, a French bishop should serve as the episcopal authority for the Catholic Church. The government itself took no official position on the matter, and turning to the wishes of the clergy serving in America, Rome felt that a superior rather than a bishop ordinary might at first fill the needs of the American Church. "Franklin's favorable view of Carroll evidently had an influence in the Marylander's appointment as superior," one commentator has noted, and "it was now understood that a future bishop should possess powers ordi-

[196] In that same year of 1808, John Carroll would, by right, become the country's first archbishop.

nary, that is, without any connection with a prelate of some foreign nation."[197]

Carroll, of course, would be that man, and his episcopal appointment came in 1790. The official announcement arrived in April of that year, and Carroll received invitations to have his consecration in such places as Quebec, Dublin, Paris, or one of the Low Countries. Instead, he chose the chapel of Lulworth Castle in Dorset, England, the ancestral home of his friend Thomas Weld and where his good friend Fr. Charles Plowden served as chaplain. Historians note that his arrival in England for the grand event coincided with a deep division in the English Catholic Church between those who supported an oath of allegiance to the civil government and those who opposed it. Interesting it was that Carroll's consecrator, Charles Walmsley, and the preacher, Plowden, were both staunch opponents of such an oath.

Such controversy was far from observable on the day itself—the feast of the Assumption of the Blessed Virgin Mary into Heaven, August 15, 1790. "Ages succeed ages," Charles Plowden reminded his congregation, "empires subvert empires, but the empire of Jesus Christ perseveres ever one and the same." Plowden noted the reason for this, that the Church was "ever persecuted and ever conquering, because all human revolutions are entirely subservient to it, and the formation of the kingdom of Christ is the ultimate object of the whole dispensation of providence in the government of this world."[198] Plowden, in a few brief sentences, stressed the growth of the Catholic Faith in America and told his hearers that "thousands are there earnestly demanding Catholic instructors, and

[197] Hanley, *American Revolution*, 184.

[198] "A Short Account of the Establishment of the New See of Baltimore in Maryland" (London: Coughlin, 1790), 6.

all penetrated with reverence for the apostolical See of St. Peter, have concurred to demand from his successor a Catholic prelate."[199] He drew a significant comparison between Pope St. Gregory the Great and England's outstanding missionary, Augustine of Canterbury, and the missionary endeavors awaiting America's new bishop, John Carroll. He concluded by commending Carroll to the Queen of Heaven and asked those in attendance to "earnestly solicit the descent of the Holy Ghost on the Bishop-elect," so that, like Augustine of Canterbury, "he may worthily fulfill the extent of the apostleship to which he is called."[200]

That apostleship was to consist of reestablishing any of the existing secular clergy, who had previously been Jesuits prior to the Society's suppression in the Church twenty-five years earlier, back into full communion with the Society, should they choose. It included also the bringing to America of Sulpicians from France and Jesuits from England to satisfy those needs Fr. Plowden referred to, the establishment of a physical plant, especially in areas where Catholic numbers were significantly growing, the purchasing of land and ultimate construction of a cathedral for his diocese—the first such in the new United States, no small feat for any man, but well accomplished by the man chosen America's first bishop.

What Bishop Carroll would preside over, and his cousin Charles Carroll of Carrollton would carefully follow, was a noticeable change in the nation's early years:

> Maryland Catholics were still thought to be wealthy, and many were. Of the nine Marylanders who owned 150 or more slaves at the time of the federal census

[199] Ibid., 6–7.
[200] Ibid., 8–9.

(1790) five were Catholics. Charles Carroll of Carrollton with 316 slaves headed the list. Daniel, the bishop's brother, had only 53. A quarter or more of those owning fifty slaves were of the bishop's faith—almost double the percentage of Catholics in the total population. By the time of the War of 1812, the old Catholic aristocracy, whose activities now centered as much in town houses as in manor houses, had absorbed new strains. The Carrolls, Darnalls, Digges, Brents, Brookes, and Neales welcomed from Ireland the Barrys, Walshes, and Tiernans and from France or Saint-Dominque the Pascaults, Chatards, and Ducatels. The position of the Catholic aristocracy was enhanced even more by its marital alliances with the European nobility ... Wealthy families continued to build and maintain chapels for the Catholics in their neighborhoods. The Carroll chapels at Doughoregan Manor and in Annapolis were the most notable, but in addition to the Boone's and Queen's chapels that survived the colonial era, the Digges, Young, Waring, Reeve, Barry and other families provided houses of worship in the Revolutionary and early national periods ... The landowning Catholic aristocrats of Maryland were Federalists to a man, as was their Archbishop. A handful of Catholic merchants, however, such as John Hillen and Luke Tiernan of Baltimore were Jeffersonians. Whether Federalist or Jeffersonian Republican, Maryland Catholics were thoroughly convinced that theirs was a land blessed by God.[201]

[201] Thomas W. Spalding, *The Premier See: A History of the Archdiocese of Baltimore, 1789–1989* (Baltimore: The Johns Hopkins University Press, 1989), 57–58.

Part 2: Statesman

Several years before the winning of independence, the Continental Congress decided that after the war, a form of unified national government must be established, and since this appeared a given, plans must begin early. A committee was established to thoroughly study the issue and devise a workable plan; such was completed and submitted to Congress through John Hancock, the devised scheme referred to as Articles of Confederation. Congress was so preoccupied with the particulars of war that debate wore on for over a year, and there was apparently significant division.

> The principle disputes raged over the questions whether taxes should be apportioned according to the gross number of inhabitants counting slaves or excluding them—the South of course wishing them excluded; whether large and small states should have equality in voting; whether Congress should be given the right to regulate Indian affairs, and whether Congress should be permitted to fix the western boundaries of those states which claimed to the Mississippi.[202]

In November 1777, Congress approved a draft and sent it to the states for ratification. It would be nearly three and one half years before the Articles became the law of the land; nine states had ratified early, but the remainder held back because of the question of Western lands. Maryland was especially conspicuous in its claim that such lands be regarded as a common possession of all the states.

[202] Wayne Andrews (ed.), *Concise Dictionary of American History* (New York: Charles Scribner's Sons, 1962), 65. See also Paul S. Boyer, *The Oxford Companion to United States History* (Oxford University Press, 2001), 51.

> To encourage army enlistments, Congress in September 1776 proposed that each state grant a bounty of land to officers and soldiers—up to five hundred acres to high-ranking officers, one hundred to each enlisted man. The Maryland convention returned a message that the state had little land it could claim as its own and could ill afford to purchase western territory to meet the request of match competition from landed states. Marylanders pointed out that if larger states claiming imperial domains could use their lands to pay their soldiers and fund their public debt as they pleased, Maryland and the other states having no such claims "must be so weakened and impoverished, that they can hold their liberties only at the will of their powerful neighbors." Taking the lead among the landless states, Maryland finally refused to ratify the Articles of Confederation until its neighbor to the south and others surrendered their western claims to the Congress and accepted definite boundaries. No state should stand in the Union as a preeminent power, Marylanders argued.[203]

The Articles provided for a "perpetual union," or a "firm league of friendship" between the states. Each state retained its sovereignty in all areas not specifically ceded to the government. It was a unicameral structure—Congress only, and each state was to send two to seven delegates, though each state, regardless of size, was to have one vote. The cost of maintaining the government was to come from a common treasury to which all the states contributed, assessed, in each case, by the value of their surveyed land. Foreign affairs, waging war, and operating a postal service were in the government's hands, but

[203] Robert J. Brugger, *Maryland: A Middle Temperament: 1634–1980* (Baltimore: The Johns Hopkins University Press, 1988), 133.

these and several powers of the Congress could not be exercised without a vote of the majority of the states. The only important powers not turned over to Congress were the "authority to raise money directly, the authority to enlist troops directly, and the authority to regulate commerce." As early as February 1780, the state of New Jersey was already calling for "amendment and invigoration of the Articles," even before they were operative.[204] Little wonder Charles Carroll could write to a cousin, informing him that, "A convention is to meet at Philadelphia next May for the purpose of revising the Articles of Confederation, correcting its defects, and enlarging the powers of Congress. The meeting, it is thought, will be full, and consist of the first characters in this country."[205]

Prior to the constitutional convention which met in Philadelphia in 1787, two conferences were held. In 1785, the Alexandria–Mount Vernon Conference was called to solve navigational problems on the Potomac, the body of water separating Maryland and Virginia; also, currency issues were resolved. The thought quickly arose that if two states can

[204] Andrews, 65–66. Interestingly, the Congress was presided over by an administrator of sorts, chosen each year. As the presiding officer of the Congress, he bore the title President of the United States. Marylander John Hanson of Mulberry Grove Plantation was the first to occupy this position, and hence, in qualified terms, he is sometimes referred to as the first President of the United States.

[205] Charles Carroll of Carrollton to Daniel Carroll of Duddington, March 13, 1787, in Rowland, 11, 105. One of Carroll's biographers, in describing the Articles of Confederation, went so far as to assert that it all went back to the lamentable fact that nearly everybody, whether he admitted it or not, "cared more about his state than he did about the country as a whole, and was still intensely conscious of the jealousy and rivalry that had held over from the time the states were colonies." Smith, 224.

discuss and solve problems, why not all? Hence, the two states invited all the rest to a conference at Annapolis in 1786, to attempt to resolve problems common to all.

The Annapolis Convention of 1786 was doomed to failure from the start; only nine states selected delegates, and five actually sent them.[206] Although little came of the gathering, at least Alexander Hamilton was there, representing New York, and he introduced a petition asking the delegates to issue a call for a further convention to be held in the city of Philadelphia the following year, for the purpose of revising, strengthening, and amending the Articles of Confederation. It was really because of this Annapolis Convention that the Constitutional Convention became a reality.

There were very few at Philadelphia who had been at the two Continental Congresses, either because they were not chosen or their political views had changed. The problems common to all delegates were power distribution. How could they move from the Articles of Confederation to federalism? They must find a proper distribution between state and national government—the two had to be balanced by a proper form of government. Hence, form and basis of authority and balance all had to be thought out and resolved.

Charles Carroll was selected a delegate to the convention but chose to decline. His cousin, Daniel Carroll of Rock Creek, the brother of Bishop John Carroll, would be one of the Maryland delegates.[207] Once arrived, the delegates set

[206] Virginia, Maryland, Pennsylvania, Delaware, and New York.

[207] The Maryland signers of the U.S. Constitution would be Daniel Carroll, James McHenry, and Daniel of St. Thomas Jenifer. Carroll, along with Thomas Fitzsimmons of Philadelphia (signing for Pennsylvania), were the only two Catholics to affix their signatures to the document.

about to answer the question: How much power would the national government have at the expense of the states? An initial resolution on May 27, 1787, called for supreme legislative, executive, and judicial branches of government—much power to the central government, which made many of the delegates suspicious of too much power centered in the federal government; with this, ideological lines were quickly drawn.

Edmund Randolph, delegate from Virginia, quickly proposed a large state plan; a bicameral legislature,[208] the lower house elected on the basis of proportional representation and the upper house elected by the lower. It was a plan that gave the federal government the power to resolve any problem between nation and state, an all-powerful government in which the legislature would select the executive and members of the judiciary. To offset this, William Patterson of New Jersey proposed a small state plan; the legislature would be unicameral,[209] sovereignty of states would hold sway, and the specific powers of the states would be clearly delineated. Both plans were a step above the Articles of Confederation because they saw the need for executive and legislative branches of government. If one accepted the Virginia Plan, one saw the New Jersey Plan as a continuation of the Articles of Confederation, and though both plans saw the national government needed more power, the smaller plan said, "Let's give it just the power it needs now," while the larger held it should be given all power it may need.

In mid-June, Alexander Hamilton proposed a stronger central government than the Virginia Plan had suggested; the heart of his program was legislative: a bicameral legisla-

[208] Upper and lower house.
[209] One house.

ture, no need for individual states, and lifetime tenure for the president, the upper house of the legislature, and the judiciary. Hamilton was trying to eliminate the deadlock by raising the tone of the debates; if he can get them to move away from dividing issues and get them to unify on something else, compromise might be the result. Most of the delegates were opposed to the Hamilton proposal, and by mid-July were ready for a compromise.

That came from Connecticut delegate Roger Sherman in the form of the Connecticut (Great) Compromise. This merely resolved the problem of representation by taking the concept of sovereignty and equality of states and said it shall apply in the Senate; in other words, each state would have an equal number of senators regardless of its size. After this, the idea of form became central, solving the main issue of power and the side issue of supremacy. In August, James Wilson of Pennsylvania said they should establish a structure on the national level just as it existed on the state level; Wilson's plan was to give the national government expressed, enumerated, delegated, and implied powers and make the state governments residual powers.[210]

Without doubt, the Virginia Plan profited more from the new government, and although the structure was federal, it needed a basis of authority—something to keep it balanced. The question was soon raised: if popular sovereignty is adequate for representation, should it not serve as a basis for a

[210] Such will be found in the Constitution, Article 1, Section 8, Clauses 1–18. Interestingly, during the course of these debates, Virginia's James Madison said the states were needed for elections, constitutional amendments, collection of taxes, and so forth, and other than that, they were of little use on the national level.

new government? Almost to a man, they agreed.[211] The form, then, would be federal, and the basis of authority, popular sovereignty.

The next problem arose of a conflict arising between nation and state—who would solve it? Several proposals were advanced to solve this question,[212] but in the end, the principle of judicial review was accepted: they give to the judicial branch a negating power. If the executive and legislative branches embark on a course of action contrary to the Constitution, the judiciary negates it. It is the judiciary which acts as a balancing agent within the governmental structure; any conflict that exists between state law and the national constitution will be resolved by the federal judiciary in con-

[211] Two delegates objected; Roger Sherman of Connecticut, a commoner who had recently risen to the well-to-do class, was distrustful of giving the people this sort of power, and George Mason of Virginia, a large property owner and well educated, believed the right to vote should be based on the sort of qualifications he and other well-to-do's had.

[212] One was Madison's idea: if a conflict arose, use force. Such would be a physical impossibility; the army was small and mostly occupied with duty on the western frontier: further, if based on force, it would never be permanent. Then the Legislative Negative was introduced: federal agents were to be appointed as observers in their respective legislatures; before state laws took effect, the agents would compare them with existing national laws—if they did not conflict, they could become operative, if not, they were invalidated. Such would maintain a balance between nation and state, but to the nation's advantage. Finally, the Executive Judicial Council of review was put forth; it would be composed of the president and a number of federal judges who would examine all national laws enacted—if they did not balance with the Constitution or existing federal law, they were returned to their house of origin for redrafting. This would also be to the advantage of national sovereignty. In the end, none of these approaches were enacted.

formity with national identity. With the form, basis of authority, and mechanism of balance, the document had its governmental structure and needed only specification.[213]

The process of ratification was a lengthy one; all of the states had lengthy debate in their respective legislatures, and political battle lines were being drawn between those fearing the governmental experiment soon to take effect would enhance the power of government to such a degree that the individual would be forgotten—or at least lost in the shuffle. On the other hand, significant elements were just as convinced that the document produced, and the new form of government to emerge, would bring about order, stability, a sound currency, national strength, and so on, of which each citizen would be a part. The two views of government as they began in these years have largely remained part and parcel of who we have become as a nation. In the late 1780s, as things were taking form, those who favored a greater emphasis on the individual, more power to the states, an agrarian emphasis in society, and a fear of centralization would come to look to Thomas Jefferson as their leader and become known first as Republicans, later as Democratic-Republicans, and finally as Democrats. The latter term endures into the twenty-first century. On the other hand, those pro-British (as opposed to pro-French) elements, favoring

[213] The basic structure of the document is the Preamble, framework of government, method for change, the process for acceptance, and the Bill of Rights. The Preamble sets out the purposes for which the government had been created, the first three articles deal with framework, Article 4 with federalism, Article 5 with the method of change, Article 6 with the supremacy clause, and Article 7 with the method of ratification—the Constitution was to become binding when it was ratified by three-fourths, or nine of the states. There followed, ultimately, the Bill of Rights.

strong centralization, more power to the federal government, a strong national currency, power in the hands of the financially successful, educated classes were called Federalists and looked to Alexander Hamilton as their leader; it was to this party that our first president under the Constitution belonged: George Washington of Virginia.

With the government officially established, the first presidential election was held in January 1789, and presidential electors were chosen in all nine states which had, up to now, ratified the Constitution. Both the House of Representatives and the United States Senate were organized in April, and in the latter body, presidential ballots were counted, unanimously choosing Washington the nation's first president.[214] The first inaugural ceremony was held on the steps of Federal Hall, at the corner of Broad and Wall Streets, New York City, and shortly after taking office, Washington received a congratulatory message from the Roman Catholics of the new nation. The document was signed by Charles Carroll, his cousin Daniel Carroll of Rock Creek, Dominic Lynch of New York, and Thomas Fitzsimmons of Philadelphia.[215] They

[214] George Washington received sixty-nine ballots, and John Adams of Massachusetts, with thirty-four, was chosen Vice President. Both men were of similar political persuasion—Federalists.

[215] Dominic Lynch (1754–1824) was a leading Catholic layman in New York. A very successful wine merchant, he had attended Georgetown College in its early years and returned to his native city to make his fortune; he eventually became Secretary of the American Society for the Encouragement of Domestic Manufactures, as well as a Director of North River Insurance Company and the New York branch of the Second Bank of the United States. He died in Paris. Thomas Fitzsimmons was an Irish born merchant, banker, and politician. A founding father of the Friendly Sons of St. Patrick in the city

began their address by apologizing to the new president for their tardiness in writing, explaining that the distance separating them made it difficult to come together and work on their thoughts in unified fashion. They told Washington that it was his peculiar talent "in war and in peace, to afford security to those who commit their protection into your hands," and even more importantly:

> You encourage respect for religion; and inculcate, by words and actions, that principle, on which the welfare of nations so much depends, that a superintending providence governs the events of the works, and watches over the conduct of men. Your exalted maxims, and unwearied attention to the moral and physical improvement of our country, have produced already the happiest effects.[216]

Change was coming to the new country rapidly, the Catholic laymen felt, and such was due in no small measure to Washington's accomplishments; they described the national prosperity now extant as pleasing to them for another reason, the fact that "we shall have a well founded title to claim from her justice, the equal rights of citizenship as the price of our blood spilt under your eyes." They concluded their statement by commending the President to the care of Divine Providence, since human means fell short of their desire for the "prolongation of your health and life, in which are included the energy of your example, the wisdom of your counsels, and the persuasive eloquence of your virtue."[217]

---

of Philadelphia, he was a leading force in the Federalist Party and an early advocate for the abolishment of the slave trade.

216 Guilday, 365.

217 Ibid., 365–366.

Washington, for his part, responded to the Catholic laymen on March 12, 1790, assuring them that he received "with much satisfaction, your congratulations" and quite optimistically shared with them that the prospected national prosperity as then seen was "truly animating" and ought to "excite the exertions of all good men, to establish and secure the happiness of their country, in the permanent duration of its freedom and independence," always, needless to say, "under the smiles of Divine Providence." Then, in an even more specific sort of praise, the Chief Executive told his friends:

> I hope ever to see America among the foremost Nations in examples of justice and Liberality. And I presume that your fellow-citizens will not forget the patriotic part, which you took in the establishment of their Revolution, and the establishment of their Government—or the important assistance, which they received from a Nation, in which the Roman Catholic Faith is professed.[218]

Washington concluded wishing "all the members of your Society in America, animated alone by the pure spirit of Christianity, and still conducting themselves as faithful subjects of our free Government ... every temporal and spiritual felicity."[219]

When historians speak of the Federalist Era in American History, they refer to the period from Washington's inauguration, through his administration and that of his one-term successor John Adams, until the so-called "last stand" of the party when they came together for the Hartford Convention of 1815. The principles of the party were paramount during

[218] Ibid., 366.
[219] Ibid.

those years until political exigencies began to eclipse what they had advanced from the earliest days of the Republic. In that vein, Charles Carroll was to be found a staunch supporter of the Federalist Party:

> The Federalists of 1791, as represented by Charles Carroll of Carrollton, had very clear views as to the Federal nature of the United States government, as the "general governments" of the States in contradiction to the "particular governments" of the "American nations." Carroll calls it a "Confederacy" and speaks of certain regulations as not likely to "endanger the tranquility of the United States or [to] involve *them* in contests with foreign nations." The very name "Federalists" was a protest against consolidation and the theory of nationality.[220]

Divisions on the nature of the federal government and its many particulars were, not surprisingly, not long in coming. Even before political parties were clearly delineated, there was the emergence of a group referred to as Anti-Federalists; such individuals believed the Constitution created an office of the presidency which had the potential of becoming a monarchy, that the new government as now constituted was far removed from the states and might abrogate, at least in part, the power of individual states, that individual rights were not sufficiently provided for in the courts, and that the Constitution should contain a bill of rights.[221] Carroll, staunchly in the opposition camp, had reason to complain to Alexander Hamilton early on about an unnamed antagonist.

[220] Rowland, 2, 177.

[221] Especially conspicuous for these views were: Patrick Henry, George Clinton, Melancton Smith, Thomas Jefferson, Samuel Adams, Richard Henry Lee, George Mason, James Winthrop, and others.

> His character I could not well see through during the time we were together. I noticed a disposition to perplex and puzzle, which left an unfavorable impression on my mind. He appeared to me not to want talents, but judgement and steadiness; and I suspect he possesses of ambition a *quantum sufficit* for any man. I hope the friends of stability, in other words the *real* friends of liberty and their country, will unite to counteract the schemes of men, who have uniformly manifested a hostile temper to the present government; the adoption of which has rescued these states from that debility and confusion and those horrors which unhappy France has experienced of late, and may still labor under.[222]

Whoever the gentleman in question, he was, for sure, one who posed some sort of threat to order and stability, and if such thinking gained a foothold in the land, Federalists saw emerging the "Great Beast—a democratic majority led around by demagogues—stalking the land."[223] Such was not their only concern, in fact:

> While the rights of property occupied a central place in Federalists' thinking, it was far from being the sum total of their philosophy. Their range of vison was more spacious: it embraced the Good Society in all its aspects, political, social, and economic. The Federalists' objective was to mold the United States in accord with their vision of an established order securely

[222] Charles Carroll of Carrollton to Alexander Hamilton, October 22, 1792, cited in ibid., 181. Carroll's references here are to the weaknesses and deficiencies in the previous Articles of Confederation, and his French reference is to the French Revolution, then at the heights of its horrors.

[223] John C. Miller, *The Federalist Era: 1789–1801* (New York: Harper & Row, 1960), 116.

> protected against demagogues and democratic majorities. This vision took the form of a highly aristocratic, class-conscious society in which gentlemen knew their privileges and the lower orders knew their place—the price, the Federalists insisted, of order, stability and progress. Federalism was not a wholly static political philosophy; it changed with the times, but its progress was not in the direction of liberalism.[224]

Charles Carroll's tenure in the United States Senate was a brief three years. The state of Maryland had passed a piece of legislation making it impermissible for public office holders to serve simultaneously in both the national legislature and the state assembly. As a result, Carroll submitted his resignation to the U.S. Senate, preferring the Maryland legislature since "he had formerly left the Continental Congress to devote himself to the works of the Maryland Senate."[225] Some historical accounts go so far as to claim that service to one's state was considered superior to the national legislature, purely because of the newness of the governmental experiment. In any event,

> Washington learned with dismay of Charles Carroll of Carrollton to give up his seat in Congress and many of his associates felt the same way … Washington wrote deploring Mr. Carroll's leaving Congress, saying "His ideas generally concur with mine." But Charles Carroll of Carrollton and most of his immediate associates felt that there was a higher degree of honor and usefulness in serving as a Maryland Senator than as a delegate in Congress.[226]

[224] Ibid., 117.
[225] Rowland, 2, 182.
[226] Leonard, 147.

Washington apparently did more than express a sentiment—he was quick to try to persuade Carroll back into the national spotlight. The nation's first president fully understood his old friend's connection to Maryland's politics, and especially the position he occupied in the Maryland legislature; nonetheless, he was quick to realize that men of Carroll's character and uprightness were oftentimes a rare commodity in political life, and the more he could exert himself on the national scene, the nation would be enhanced, not to mention the Federalist Party. This mindset also extended to many in the party. Although Washington seemed an almost unanimous choice to be the first citizen to hold the office of president, his first term saw significant discord, much division between political parties, stemming from the major differences that had emerged between Thomas Jefferson and his political rival, Alexander Hamilton.

A look at these differences is very revealing of party differences on a whole:

> Jeffersonian principles embraced (1) a democratic agrarian order based on the individual freeholder; (2) a broad diffusion of wealth; (3) relative freedom from industrialism, urbanism, and organized finance; (4) sympathy for debtor interests; (5) distrust of centralized government; (6) belief in the perfectibility of man; (7) confidence in the view that the people, acting through representative institutions, could be left to govern themselves. Hamiltonian principles included (1) a balanced and diversified economic order; (2) active governmental encouragement of finance, industry, commerce, and shipping; (3) sympathy for creditor interests; (4) advocacy of a strong national government under executive leadership; (5) distrust of

> the people's capacity to govern; and (6) a belief that the best government was that of an elite.[227]

Up until the last minute it was unclear, in 1792, if Washington would run for a second term. If so, almost certainly he would face no opposition for the nomination within his own Federalist Party, for while his administration had experienced interior difficulties and tensions, his prestige among the American people was still very high. On the other side, Jefferson was politically strong, and growing stronger quickly. If any other Federalist were to be the candidate, it is likely the sage of Monticello would have run against him. Curiously, Alexander Hamilton received a letter from a friend, suggesting that if the President chose not to run, Charles Carroll should be the nominee,[228] while Hamilton, for his part, replied that he was quite sure Washington intended to present himself for a second term, but, "if it turns out otherwise, I say unequivocally—I will cooperate in running the gentleman you mention, as one of the two who are to fill the two great offices. Which of the two may turn up *first* or *second*, must be an affair of some casualty as the Constitution stands. My real respect and esteem for the character brought into view will insure him my best wishes in every event."[229] Although it is almost inconceivable to think that a Catholic could be nominated for president

[227] Richard B. Morris, *Encyclopedia of American History* (New York: Harper & Row, 1965), 123–124.

[228] James McHenry to Alexander Hamilton, October 20, 1792, cited in Smith, 246.

[229] Ibid. Smith, in her footnote indicates that the letter from McHenry encloses these words in quotes and states they are from Hamilton's reply to McHenry "of the 10th ultimo." She cites as her source John C. Hamilton, *Works of Alexander Hamilton*, V, 536. See also McDermott, 208.

on either party in 1792, let alone elected to the office, some historical conjecture has been put forth that with Hamilton's support, Carroll could easily have been nominated and might well have defeated Jefferson in the general election.[230]

History has portrayed Charles Carroll as a staunch party man, an ardent Federalist. To be sure, he was loyal to his party affiliation—too many sources bear this out. At the same time, he was quick to register his disagreement when he felt it necessary, and, on the whole, he appears to have had a low opinion of political parties in general. Writing to a British friend, he noted that "we have political parties amongst us but they are too trivial and of too little consequence for me to relate or you to hear," and he added that the reason for the existence of such factions did not differ substantially from the same sort of divisions which existed in England, namely "the want of a sufficient number of lucrative offices to gratify the avarice or the ambition of the 'Outs.'"[231] Years later, he went further, expressing his belief that, "If our country should continue to be a sport of parties ... anarchy will follow."[232]

If those in the Federalist camp were scandalized with events unfolding in France, they were even more so with the

[230] Smith, 246.

[231] Charles Carroll of Carrollton to Edmund Jennings, November 3, 1765, cited in Field, 98.

[232] Charles Carroll of Carrollton to James McHenry, November 4, 1800, cited in Smith, 249. A significant reason for the sharp division in political parties in the United States was the French Revolution. One historian has noted that the Revolution "widened the cleavage between the Federalists and their antagonists," adding that, "At its outset, the French Revolution had enlisted the sympathy of most Americans; but with the proclamation of the French Republic (Sept. 21, 1792) and the execution of Louis XVI (Jan. 21), American opinion began to divide sharply." Morris, 125.

sudden rise in popularity of the Democratic-Republicans (or simply Republicans) headed by Thomas Jefferson. Many in the party were alarmed with Jefferson's views and his increasing influence. Once speaking of a rebellion in Massachusetts, he said that, "No country should be long without one,"[233] and Carroll biographers note that the Marylander had once seen a letter written by Jefferson expressing his belief that "to preserve the liberties of a people, a revolution once in a century was necessary."[234]

To be sure, Carroll distrusted Jefferson as much as his fellow Federalists, though on the question of loyalty to France, he deviated from his party somewhat by agreeing with those who reminded the public that the United States, as then known, might never have come into existence had it not been for the help of France.[235]

The issue came to the forefront again during the Citizen Genet affair of 1793. In April of that year, Edmund Charles Genet, Minister of the French Republic, had arrived in Charleston, South Carolina, with instructions to negotiate a new treaty of commerce with the United States, replacing the one signed during the American Revolution.[236] Even before presenting his credentials, he commissioned four privateers to spy on British vessels along the coastal waters of the United States, and went even further, organizing, on American soil,

[233] Thomas Jefferson to James Madison, December 20, 1787, cited in Smith, 250.

[234] Charles Carroll of Carrollton to Alexander Hamilton, April 18, 1800, cited in ibid.

[235] Carroll, himself a fluent French speaker, whose early education had centered in Paris and other French cities, may well have identified with this position for such reasons, not to mention France's profession of the Catholic Faith.

[236] The Treaty of Amity and Commerce of 1778.

expeditions against Spanish and British territories. Small wonder that President Washington received him coolly, and, within a matter of weeks, had him presented with a communication stating that his actions had constituted an infringement of American sovereignty. He was also told that the privateers he commissioned would have to leave American waters, and, though he promised to comply, he simply went on, authorizing the arming of *The Little Sarah*, a ship brought in by a French vessel, with plans to be refitted as *La Petite Démocrate*. He threatened to take his case directly to the people after being threatened against dispatching the vessel.

Washington held to neutrality in the case, inciting the wrath of the Anti-Federalist, Democratic-Republican press, who strongly supported Genet. At the same time, Alexander Hamilton wrote a series of articles, using the pen name "Pacificus," defending the President's position and his right to decide the matter. A reply came from James Madison, using the penname "Helvidius," a writing on behalf of himself and Jefferson to say that Genet's conduct and poor judgment had harmed their political cause. Washington's cabinet had voted to demand Genet's recall, and by now, the Jacobins had taken control in France and issued a warrant for his arrest. Washington, however, refused to extradite the Frenchman, and he went on to become an American citizen.[237]

[237] The Jacobins, or *Société des Jacobins, de la liberté de l'Égalité*, were the most influential political club during the French Revolution of 1789. The period of their political ascendancy included the Reign of Terror, during which over ten thousand people were put on trial and executed in France, many for political crimes. Genet, for his part, eventually married a daughter of Governor George Clinton of New York.

Carroll did not entirely agree with Washington in his handling of the Genet Affair, largely because of his propensity to things French. The President had tried to explain his course of action to his Maryland friend, observing that, "Every true friend to this country must see and feel that the policy of it is not to embroil ourselves with any nation whatever, but to avoid their disputes and their politics; and if they will harass one another to avail ourselves of the neutral conduct we have adopted."[238]

Interestingly, Carroll was sometime later under consideration to be named U.S. Minister to France, succeeding James Monroe. Carroll had made it clear that he did not want to return to service on the national level but was more than content to render service to his native state in the Maryland Senate. Even Washington picked up this reluctance when he wrote that, "Mr. Carroll of Carrollton, though sensible and attached to Federalist measures, would find himself on quite new ground, and besides, he has such large concerns of his own to attend to, and is so tenacious of them, that it is morally certain he would not be prevailed on to go."[239]

Some historians hold the view that the Federalists would not have been successful in 1796 had it not been for the rise of Napoleon in France, this on top of the revolutionary events that had defined so much of the country with its secularity, hatred of the Church, and attempts to totally overthrow the existing culture, mores, and political framework of government. Napoleon's exploits, wrote one commentator, "were so extensive and brilliant as to alarm even those who

[238] George Washington to Charles Carroll of Carrollton, May 1, 1796, cited in Rowland, 11, 205–206.

[239] George Washington to Timothy Pickering, July 8, 1796, cited in Smith, 254.

had espoused everything French."[240] Looking ahead to the election, Charles Carroll wrote that "the friends of government dread the election of Jefferson."[241] Carroll supported Adams, and the final count elected him over Jefferson, who, with the second highest number, became Vice President.

Much turmoil followed in Adams's administration, and the bipartisanship he had hoped for never seemed to become a reality. In 1798, the Alien and Sedition Acts were passed, the first ordering out of the country all aliens regarded as dangerous to the public peace or even suspected of "treasonable or secret inclinations," the latter making it a "high misdemeanor, punishable by fine and imprisonment, for citizens or aliens to enter into unlawful combinations opposing execution of the national laws" to hinder any federal official from performing his duty, or any attempt to aid "any insurrection, riot, unlawful assembly, or combination."[242] The legislation was intended to suppress any political opposition, and some twenty-five persons were prosecuted, with ten being convicted—all of them Republican editors or printers. Somewhat in response to this were the Kentucky and Virginia Resolutions, the first being written by Jefferson, the second by Madison, and both invoking the compact theory of government in their insistence that the Alien and Sedition Acts were unconstitutional. The Kentucky Resolutions, by far the more forceful of the two, held that in areas where the national government exercised powers not specifically granted to it, each state "has an equal right to judge for itself, as well of infractions as of the mode and measure of redress."

[240] Ibid.

[241] Charles Carroll of Carrollton to James McHenry, December 5, 1796, cited in McDermott, 213.

[242] Morris, 29.

The Virginia Resolutions stated that in such cases, the states "have the right and are in duty bound to interpose for arresting the progress of the evil."[243] Partisanship had surely come to the forefront, and the Federalists were to have a harder and harder time hanging on to power.

The century's final year, 1799, witnessed the death of George Washington, father of his country and revered by his countrymen, Catholics every bit as much as their fellow Americans. His good friend Carroll, then a member of the Maryland Senate, along with Uriah Forrest, a distinguished state senator from St. Mary's County, were assigned the task of formerly presenting the Maryland House of Delegates a formal resolution from the Senate, proposing a day of "mourning, humiliation and prayer" throughout the state. Rodger Brooke Taney, the future Catholic Chief Justice of the Supreme Court, then serving his first year in the House of Delegates from Calvert County, left a memory of the event:

> General Washington died while the Legislature was still in session. The news reached Annapolis in the evening, and the next morning, when the House met, almost every countenance looked sad, and nothing else was spoken of. Immediately after the Houses were organized, the Senate sent down a message to the House of Delegates proposing to pay appropriate honors. Charles Carroll of Carrollton and ... [Uriah Forrest] two of the most distinguished men in Maryland were appointed by the Senate to bring the message, and I never witnessed a more impressive scene. The two honored Senators with their gray locks, stood at the bar of the House with tears rolling down their cheeks. The Speaker and members rose to receive them, and stood while the message was

[243] Ibid., 130.

> delivered. It was no empty formal pageant. It was the outward sign of the grief within, and few were present who did not shed tears on the occasion. My eyes, I am sure, were not dry.[244]

The Carroll family's eulogistic literature on the nation's first president was given very public utterance by Charles' cousin, Baltimore's Bishop John Carroll, also a good friend of Washington. In December of 1799, the Bishop had written a pastoral letter to the faithful of his diocese, recommending that Washington's birthday, February 22, 1800, be set aside as a day of mourning throughout the diocese. On that day, in St. Peter's pro-cathedral in Baltimore, a memorial service was conducted, at which Carroll preached. Taking the eighth chapter of the Book of Wisdom as his text, he showed the Founding Father, the *pater patriae,* had been uniquely chosen by God to shepherd the colonies through the years leading to their departure from the mother country:

> To superintend the movements, and operations of such a revolution; to control, during its progress, jealousies, enmities, suspicions, and other conflicting passions; and from their collision, to educe national and individual prosperity, peace, order, liberty and regular government; required the discernment and masterly contrivance of that Supreme Director and Artist, who unites together the links, and holds in his hands the chain of all human events. Contemplating as much as is allowed to feeble mortals, his divine agency in preparing the means and conducting the progress of the American revolution, we may presume to say, that

[244] Samuel Tyler, *Memoir of Rodger Brooke Taney* (Baltimore: John Murphy & Co., 1872), 85. Cited in Rowland, 11, 233.

heaven impressed a character on the life of Washington, and a temper on his soul, which eminently qualified him to bear the most conspicuous part, and be its principal instrument in accomplishing this stupendous work … May these United States flourish in pure and undefiled religion, in morality, peace, union, liberty and the enjoyment of their excellent Constitution, as long as respect, honour and veneration shall gather round the name of Washington; that is, whilst there shall be any surviving record of human events.[245]

[245] Cited in Charles Carroll Carter et al., *Creating Capitol Hill: Place, Proprietors, and People* (Washington, DC: The United States Capitol Historical Society, 2018), 29. See also Guilday, 744–747.

CHAPTER 5

THE SAGA CONTINUES

After the death of Washington, and the demise of the Federalist Party, Carroll's future in the Jeffersonian period was, at best, doubtful.

> Washington's and Carroll's fates differed as concerns longevity, but not when it came to politics. Though Carrollton outlived the General by thirty-two years, his political career did not survive the *pater patriae's* death. Neither man's virtues had any place in American politics after 1800.[246]

A significant social and cultural upheaval occurred in the United States as the nineteenth century emerged, the results of which diminished so much of the "old world" in which the Federalists had been so comfortable. Among the strongest contributors to a change of thought were the French *philosophes*, with their emphasis on the perfection of the environment; democracy, science, and rationalistic education were the means to achieve this perfection, as were the teaching of modern languages (as opposed to the classical, or dead, languages),

[246] McDermott, 214.

and the study of classic liberal thought. As most upheavals, this current emphasis would be slow in emerging; anti-intellectualism characterized the majority of Americans, but inroads were being made. In time, a "savagely competitive materialistic economic order" would prevail and would be not terribly distinguishable from other aspects of society, namely the "cerebral climate … affected by the eighteenth century's ideas of benevolence, morality and classical simplicity, compounded with what was thought of as a primitive or a purified Christianity."[247] There was initially a reaction to all this, a sort of Protestant fundamentalist response. Strangely, this coincided with the inauguration of Thomas Jefferson as the third President of the United States in 1801, and yet, aside from the new President and his immediate circle:

> Few people … dreamed of separating sacred and profane learning at any level. Professors were nearly all clergymen, Federalists and orthodox in their opposition to Jefferson, Unitarianism, deism, skepticism, scriptural criticism, and religious equality.[248]

Jefferson was indeed a deist, a self-made theologian of sorts, who felt that, "Saint Paul had corrupted Christianity to prove Christ divine." A far better approach, he felt, was to "apply reason to the Book of Nature in order to discover the laws of God."[249] Though always in certain matters liberal, he had served as Washington's Secretary of State. At first, their relationship had been quite cordial, but as the years progressed, considerably cooler. By 1796, during the fierce debate

[247] Marshall Smelser, *The Democratic Republic: 1801–1815* (New York: Harper & Row, 1968), 31, 25.

[248] Ibid., 25.

[249] Ibid., 8.

over the Jay Treaty between the United States and England, he became the real leader of the Anti-Federalist opposition.[250] At least one historian feels that,

> If the French Revolution had not caused a recanvass of fundamental libertarian principles, he and his supporters probably would not have pulled off the electoral coup of 1800. Nor was his election a victory for infidel rationalism. It was the counterattack of the theologically conservative farmers against the Federalists' aristocratic contempt for America's sunburned agricultural drudges.[251]

With such background, it is not difficult to see how those of Charles Carroll's standing would increasingly feel their world passing away—modernity seemed on the ascent, and little could be done to halt its advance. It was also to be a period in which Carroll's religion would experience the first signs of what would be phenomenal growth and develop from an aristocratic minority to the Church of the poor immigrants who would, in turn, bequest to their offspring the benefits of the American promise. For now, however, chiefly a minority,

> with small reinforcements, on the perimeter, of French and Irish. Culturally the Catholics were indistinguishably American. The three marked qualities of

[250] The Jay Treaty averted war with the British, resolved certain issues remaining since the Treaty of Paris of 1783 (which had ended the Revolutionary War and brought about a decade of peaceful trade between the two nations in the midst of the French Revolution). The treaty angered France and strongly divided Americans, and there came into being sharp differences between pro-treaty Federalists and anti-treaty Democratic-Republicans.

[251] Smelser, 10.

> American Catholicism in 1801 were … its full membership in the Anglo-American culture … the attempt—eventually successful—to assert episcopal authority over lay trustees in ecclesiastical concerns; and … its freedom from foreign intrigues, a freedom made plain by Rome's acceptance of Bishop John Carroll for the American primacy, when nominated by the few American priests.[252]

Some historians feel that Charles Carroll, staunch Federalist that he was, became even more entrenched in his convictions as the administrations of Jefferson and later James Madison unfolded. There is nothing difficult to see in this, especially when news of events in France during the Revolution began to be known in America. Executions, persecutions, massacres, and all associated with the ferment taking place in a country which for centuries had been known as the eldest daughter of the Church filled many with sorrow. One biographer, considering Carroll's strong Catholicism, described him as "shocked and mortified by the treatment to which the Church and her clergy were subjected."[253]

In 1799, Napoleon Bonaparte had made himself dictator of France, assuming the title First Consul. Carroll never ceased to hope for his downfall—for the sake of liberty, peace, and most of all, world order. The Signer was never so enamored with England that he formed an ironclad attachment to her; nonetheless, he felt it of vital importance to ally America with the former mother country to bring about a decisive defeat of the French dictator. He considered both

[252] Thomas T. McAvoy, "The Catholic Minority in the United States, 1789–1821," United States Catholic Historical Society, *Records and Studies*, XXXIX–XL (1952), 33–50, cited in ibid., 33.

[253] Gurn, 201.

the third and fourth Presidents to be duped by Napoleon, and prey who could easily be manipulated. Early on in Jefferson's first term, Carroll wrote to a friend that some of this attraction may come from his attraction to rational, scientific inquiry, or, better put, deism. "Jefferson and his chief partisans at the seat of government may pretend to be disgusted with [Thomas] Paine, but that they are really so I do not believe." He goes on to note that some of Paine's latest publications injured their cause within their own party, "but his political principles are approved by all of them, and his abuse of Washington, by several, and I fear very many of them approve his blasphemous writings against the Christian religion."[254] Friend of Washington as he was for many years, Charles Carroll was not only disturbed by Paine's writings but surely felt that in opposing the policies of the Democratic-Republicans, he was carrying out an opposition which the Father of his Country would have strongly approved.

[254] Ibid., 203. The letter cited was dated December 14, 1802, but Gurn does not disclose its recipient. Thomas Paine (1737–1809) was an English-born American founding father, political activist, philosopher, political theorist, and revolutionary. He is remember for such works as *Common Sense, The American Crisis*, and *Rights of Man*. His books played a very significant role in inspiring the patriots in 1776 to declare independence from Great Britain. His ideas reflected Enlightenment-era ideals of human rights, advocated deism, promoted reason and free thought, and argued against religion in general, and the doctrines of Christianity in particular. He once published a bitter, open letter to George Washington, whom he denounced as incompetent and a hypocrite. He advocated the right of people to overthrow their government and was singled out with a writ for his arrest. He quickly fled to France in 1792, where many considered him a great hero. Returning to the United States, he died in 1809, and, curiously, only six people attended his funeral, principally because of his criticism of Christianity.

The Louisiana Purchase had also occurred early in Jefferson's first term. In 1762, France had ceded Louisiana to Spain, but by 1800, a secret treaty had returned the territory to the French. Napoleon had in mind the creation of a French colonial empire in North America, something which concerned Jefferson because of the threat posed to American security by an imperial, aggressive power. Also, there was the fear that French possession of New Orleans might result in the closing of the Mississippi to Western commerce. Jefferson instructed the American Minister at Paris, Robert R. Livingston, to negotiate for a tract of land on the lower Mississippi for use as a port, or, failing that, a guarantee from the French of free navigation on the river. At a certain point, Napoleon gave up his grandiose scheme of colonization, and negotiations for purchase of the entire territory began in earnest. Louisiana was purchased for fifteen million—slightly more than eleven million for the land, and the remainder to cover the debts owed by France to U.S. citizens, which the American government assumed. The purchase doubled the area of the United States by the acquisition of some 828 thousand square miles lying between the Mississippi and the Rocky Mountains. Although some lack of clarity remained in the document itself, and further treaties were necessary to further clarify, the staggering addition to the United States carried great importance not only to the government in Washington but also to the Catholic Church.

One of the greatest fears in Charles Carroll's mind was that once peace had been declared between England and France, the latter (and Napoleon in particular) would seize on the newly acquired territory and deprive the United States of that which she had legitimately purchased. "What is to stop him," Carroll wrote to a friend, "we are totally unprepared for war and likely to remain so."[255] Much of the cause for this Carroll happily blamed on the Democratic-Republicans. He felt many of them to be contemptible and lacking in good faith, men who would apparently do anything to keep themselves in power. "The Democrats are a servile and timid crew," he declared to a friend, "and to keep themselves in place they would make a treaty with the devil himself, and would break it as soon as their interests might seem to render its breach subservient to their schemes."[256]

Things had never really resolved themselves in America's relations with England since the signing of the Treaty of Paris in 1783, and the country had been teetering on the verge of another conflict for several years. Federalists had consistently hoped such conflict could be averted, but their own political situation and numbers were lessening, and their strength was not nearly that of earlier years. Both Jefferson and Madison had considerable hostility to the former mother country, and in 1807, such antagonism grew when a British ship, the *Leopard*, impressed four sailors from a defenseless American vessel, the *Chesapeake*, after an attack in which three Americans were killed and eighteen wounded. A "paper blockade," which the United States considered illegal, and a series of Orders in Council followed from Britain; at the same time, Indians living on the Western fron-

[255] Ibid., 205. Throughout these years, the Napoleonic Wars were being fought, a continuation of the wars of the French Revolution. Great Britain and France fought for European supremacy and treated weaker powers heavy-handedly. The letter cited above was written in 1806, though again, Gurn offers no recipient's name nor the specific date of the letter. It was reprinted in the *American Catholic Historical Researches,* 1901, from the Dreer Collection, Pennsylvania Historical Society.

[256] Ibid., January 16, 1807, but no recipient listed.

tier had been defending their right of settlement with British guns and powder—the Battle of Tippecanoe saw the loss of some two hundred frontiersmen and afforded the War Hawks in Congress much ammunition for their strident war cries.[257] "The administration of this country has got us into a miserable hobble, from which nothing can extricate us but England's declaring war against us," Charles Carroll wrote to his son-in-law, "notwithstanding the manifold provocations given by our government, and its manifest partiality for France, the English cabinet is too wise to help our rulers out of the scrape by declaring war against the United States."[258]

England had made public apology for the *Chesapeake-Leopard* incident and was on the verge of repealing its Orders in Council, when the United States declared war on her on June 19, 1812. Needless to say, Carroll not only disapproved but was insistent on his position about the misery "our present wicked administration" had brought upon the country.[259] Carroll inquired of his son-in-law in 1813 how long the war could go on: "Can it be prosecuted without the means, and against the general bent of the nation? In consequence of the President's recommendation, an entire stop, I suppose, will be put to exports from this country. Will the people long submit to such privations? Their folly or corruption in the

[257] The War Hawks were young, energetic politicians, mostly from the South and West, who initiated legislation designed to steer the United States toward war. Leaders of the group would be such as Henry Clay of Kentucky, John C. Calhoun of South Carolina, and Felix Grundy of Tennessee.

[258] Charles Carroll of Carrollton to Robert Goodloe Harper, January 21, 1812, in Rowland, 11, 289.

[259] Charles Carroll of Carrollton to Charles Carroll of Homewood, December 5, 1813, in ibid., 298.

re-election of Mr. Madison must now be manifest."[260] Rioting had occurred in Baltimore following an attack on the offices of a newspaper, *The Federal Republican*, known for its criticisms on the Madison administration's handling of the war, and its actions in general bringing war about. Such provoked Carroll to write that, "The late occurrences in Baltimore and the temper of this government render a residence insecure in this State, and I may want all the sums I can command to enable me to move out of it, if the state of politics does not grow better, and men be suffered to speak their sentiments on the measures of the present rulers of our country and to take what newspapers they please."[261]

When the nation's capital fell into the hands of the British and so many of its buildings, including the White House, were burned, it seemed Baltimore would be next in line to be pillaged. It was of interest to the British because it was a commercial center and a port where many ships had done their part to make the British navy uncomfortable. British naval intelligence felt Baltimore would be easy prey following Washington, but on September 11, 1814, the British were routed because of a concerted effort to guard the city; they were not, however, defeated. Following their failed attempt, they turned their attention to Fort McHenry, south of Baltimore, and opened fire on the morning of September 13. Once again, Americans withheld British attempts, quickening the time to war's end.[262]

[260] Charles Carroll of Carrollton to Robert Goodloe Harper, March 4, 1813, in ibid., 295.

[261] Charles Carroll of Carrollton to Charles Carroll of Homewood, August 5, 1812, in ibid., 291–292.

[262] "During the bombardment, a young Marylander watched from one of the British ships, which he had boarded in order to try

Britain and the United States signed the Treaty of Ghent on Christmas Eve of 1814, ending the conflict, and, coincidentally, only a matter of months later, Europe and the rest of the world witnessed the downfall of Napoleon Bonaparte at the Battle of Waterloo. With his menacing presence removed, and victory in the War of 1812, an era of peace and growing prosperity seemed to be emerging for the United States. How long would it last? Charles Carroll was of the opinion it would depend,

> on the adherence to the principles which laid the foundation of its growing prosperity; the confederation of these States, sovereign and independent within the powers not generated to the general confederacy, their incorporation with that surviving and controlling government, also sovereign and independent as to the powers devolved on it by the confederacy, is a curious and complicated piece of mechanism of which the world has had no example; time will discover how long it will go on without derangement.[263]

It is difficult to say how frequently Charles Carroll had contact with his cousin, Baltimore's archbishop, with whom many historians feel he attended Bohemia Manor as young boys,

---

to effect the release of a friend. Francis Scott Key was not then famous, though Baltimoreans knew him as a promising lawyer … Young Mr. Key had an aptitude for verse making; now he reached into his pocket for something to write on and scribbled hurriedly, before he should forget the words that came into his mind: 'O say can you see, by the dawn's early light …' " Smith, 287. Key's sister, Ann Phoebe Carlton Key, was the wife of Roger B. Taney, the first Catholic Chief Justice of the Supreme Court, who handed down the Dred Scott decision.

[263] Charles Carroll of Carrollton to Elizabeth Caton Stafford, February 26, 1828, in Field, 210–211.

with whom he sailed for Europe and where the two spent years of study at the school of the English Jesuits at St. Omer in French Flanders, with whom he undertook a diplomatic mission to Canada at the time of the American Revolution, and with whom he corresponded on a variety of topics throughout his life. The news of Archbishop John Carroll's death in 1815 must have saddened his cousin, and, being the nation's first Catholic prelate, it came as a great loss to Catholics throughout his archdiocese and the entire nation. One of his biographers summed up the day of his funeral:

> The body of the Archbishop of Baltimore lay in state for two days at St. Peter's where he had so often addressed his flock. On Tuesday, surmounted by his mitre and his pastoral crozier, John Carroll was placed in his coffin. The solemn Mass of requiem was sung, and then the procession began to move slowly through Saratoga Street, up Franklin to the chapel of St. Mary's Seminary on Paca Street where the first dignitary of the Church of the United States was laid to rest. The windows along the way were thronged with spectators, and distinctions of rank and wealth, of religious opinion were laid aside as the impressive cortege wound its way through the silent streets. He lay in the vault of the beautiful little seminary where Mother Seton had first appeared in the habit of the Sisters of Charity of Saint Joseph, and there he stayed until the cathedral of Baltimore was ready to receive him, and then in 1824 John Carroll was taken to his present resting place.[264]

[264] Annabelle Melville, *John Carroll of Baltimore: Founder of the American Catholic Hierarchy* (New York: Charles Scribner's Sons, 1955), 284. St. Peter's was the oldest Catholic church and the residence of the Archbishop; the Tuesday referred to in the citation would have been December 5, 1815.

Carroll was succeeded by his coadjutor, Leonard Neale, a descendant of a prominent English Catholic Southern Maryland family whose two brothers were also priests. A former president of Georgetown, he had helped Carroll in the administration of the vast diocese since 1800 and was the first bishop to be consecrated in the United States. Neale's health rapidly began to fail, and his coadjutor, Ambrose Maréchal was appointed in July 1817. Neale had died one month before the official news arrived, and Maréchal immediately succeeded him as Archbishop. Born in France, he had entered the Sulpicians there and came to the United States at the height of the French Revolution. He and Charles Carroll had built up a considerable friendship through the years, and the Signer wrote to Baltimore's new archbishop in 1817 to congratulate him and to request he send him a chaplain who would reside with him at Annapolis, his city residence, and also while he stayed at Doughoregan Manor. Carroll expressed the wish that the priest "be a person of some literature and of mild and cheerful temper; in short, a companion of an old man to relieve those solitary hours which I shall frequently experience in the absence of my children and my grandchildren, for as I advance in years, I feel less disposition to go into company."[265]

[265] Charles Carroll of Carrollton to Archbishop Ambrose Maréchal, January 31, 1818, cited in Gurn, 215. Toward the end of the same year, Carroll wrote to the Archbishop again, highly pleased anticipating a visit from the latter. The Baltimore prelate had apparently made a request of some sort of the Signer, since Carroll said that "what little influence I may have with some of the members of the Legislature shall be exerted to obtain the object mentioned in your letter; but it will be necessary that some responsible characters of our religion from Baltimore should attend the Legislature *at the commencement of the session* to point out the reasonableness, indeed the necessity, of compliance with their petition." Charles Carroll of Carrollton to Archbishop Ambrose Marechal, December 19, 1818, cited in ibid.

Carroll was much aware of events on the national scene, and in the year 1820, the Missouri Compromise Bill was being very hotly debated. When the territories of Missouri and Maine applied to Congress for statehood, the country had twenty-two states, eleven free and eleven slave. Up to now, the political balance had been maintained by alternately admitting one free state, followed by one slave, and so on. Despite this seeming equality, the slave states had only eighty-one votes in the House of Representatives, as opposed to one hundred five for the free states; additionally, the North was growing, population-wise, at a far more rapid pace. To preserve the sectional balance, the South looked to its equal vote in the U.S. Senate.

The Missouri Territory, as then constituted, compromised all of the Louisiana Purchase, excepting that area which became the state of Louisiana in 1812 and the then-existing Arkansas Territory. The application by the Missouri Territorial Legislature for admission as a state raised the question of the legality of slavery in Missouri and in the rest of the territory west of the Mississippi. There were between two and three thousand slaves in the Upper Louisiana Country, where slavery had gone back to the days of Spanish and French colonization. From early 1819, a series of compromise amendments were introduced, debated, and each in turn defeated.[266] The result, one year later, was the final settlement, by which Missouri would be admitted as a slave state, Maine a free state, and slavery excluded from the Louisiana Purchase north of the line of thirty-six degrees thirty minutes. While the debate was prolonged, and watched closely by the entire nation, Carroll felt it was not the most pressing issue the country had

[266] The Tallmadge, Taylor, and Thomas Amendments. See Morris, 159–160.

to contend with—writing to his son-in-law, he noted that "economy is said to be the order of the day at Washington ... such a waste of time on the Missouri question is certainly incompatible with that order. The ardor and perseverance with which the debate is pursued give room to suspect that something else than the exclusion of slaves from the Missouri State is at the bottom."[267]

While it can only be guessed what Carroll had in mind by his use of "something else," the latter does give rise to the Signer's thoughts on the institution of slavery. His opposition to it became evident as early as 1797 while a member of the Maryland Assembly.[268] What caused him criticism was his presidency of the American Colonization Society in 1832. The object of this organization was to encourage blacks to emigrate to Africa, specifically to Liberia, with the hope of living a far better life than many believed they ever could in the United States. Leading the criticism was William Lloyd Garrison, generally considered the father of the abolitionist movement in the United States.[269] In 1832, in his book *Thoughts on African Colonization,* he strongly decried the organization and its leaders, Carroll and his predecessor, Bushrod Washington.[270] Referring to Carroll, he lamented the fact that he was "lauded beyond measure as a partier, a philanthropist, and a Christian!"[271] Granted Charles Carroll was a large slave owner, but as one of his early biographers noted, "if all the slaves in the Southland

[267] Charles Carroll of Carrollton to Robert Goodloe Harper, February 17, 1820, cited in Gurn, 216.

[268] McDermott, 210–211.

[269] The publication of Garrison's paper, *The Liberator,* on January 1, 1831, is generally considered to be the beginning of the abolitionist movement, formally structured.

[270] Bushrod was George Washington's nephew.

[271] Cited in Gurn, 269.

were treated as well as his, there would have been little cause for complaint. His interest in the welfare of the colored folk was as sincere as it could well be, and nothing would have pleased him better than the discovery of some practical method whereby the slaves of America might be set free."[272] The biographer went on to observe that Garrison was obviously unaware that Carroll was of an anti-slavery mind before he was born.

Shortly after Carroll's death in 1832, his son-in-law Richard Caton sought to clarify his father-in-law's position in a letter to Philadelphia's *National Gazette.* He addressed the letter to the Select and Common Councils of the city, acknowledging their statements of condolences on the death of the Signer:

> There is one trait of character in the history of Mr. Carroll's life which is not known generally, and I hope you will pardon me in taking this occasion to mention it. He bitterly lamented the existence of slavery, which British laws and policy had rooted in Maryland. He held many slaves, and he would have gladly have adopted any means by which the country could have been relieved from the evil, without inflicting a greater one in the attempt. To accomplish this, he in 1797 introduced into the Senate of Maryland a bill for a gradual abolition, the provisions of which were that the state should buy up all the female children, educate them for freedom and usefulness and bind them out, to be free at twenty-eight years of age, when habits of order would have befitted them for a state of liberty. At a given period all males, and others under forty-five years, were to be free. Had it prevailed, the measure at this period would nearly have extinguished slavery in Maryland. He never was an advocate of letting loose

[272] Ibid.

> on society a race of beings, who, nine out of ten, are incapable of providing for themselves, as he knew the experiment, often tried, had never succeeded, and he thought no one had a right to do an evil to society by such a measure. But he did all that could be done to the African race whilst in servitude; he had them protected with humanity, and he elevated their characters by religious instruction, which was daily administered by persons appointed for that purpose. The children of his colored females were daily congregated and taught their catechism, and received moral instruction. These preparatory measures he thought would advance them for a state of manumission, which must soon take place in Maryland.[273]

A significant event in Carroll's life occurred on July 4, 1820. A grand celebration was held in the city of Baltimore. A procession through the city streets celebrating the winning of American independence witnessed the now venerable Signer carrying a copy of the document to which he had affixed his signature on August 2, 1776, and receiving the congratulations of a city filled with pride. One account captured the moment:

> The grand celebration of the anniversary of the Declaration of Independence at Baltimore on Tuesday last, received a high degree of interest from the presence of Charles Carroll of Carrollton, one of the four survivors of those who signed that far-framed instrument; he took a part in the procession, supported by Colonel John E. Howard and General

[273] Richard Caton to *The National Gazette,* December 20, 1832, cited in ibid., 270.

> Samuel Smith, who maintained with their swords what the Congress decreed.[274]

Around this same time, John H.B. Latrobe, a prominent lawyer and inventor, and the son of architect Benjamin Latrobe, who designed the Basilica of the Assumption in Baltimore, met Carroll at this point in his life and observed that "his manners were charming, his countenance pleasant and sprightly, and as one looked at Mr. Carroll one saw a shadow from past days, when manner was cultivated as essential to a gentleman. He gives instances of his exactness in business matters, which, however, do not indicate that he was of a miserly disposition."[275]

The year 1824 was memorable for at least two events in Charles Carroll's life, the first being his participation in the visit of the Marquis de Lafayette to the United States. Lafayette, a French aristocrat, was a general in the American Revolutionary War, as well as a leader of the Garde Nationale during the French Revolution. As the fiftieth anniversary of the declaration of America's independence from the mother country Great Britain was approaching, Congress and the American people welcomed the famous Frenchman back as a national hero in the struggle that won our freedom. The Marquis was hosted at countless receptions, dinners, and

[274] *Niles Weekly Register*, July 8, 1820, cited in ibid., 218. The other three surviving signers, in addition to Carroll, were John Adams, Thomas Jefferson, and William Floyd of New York.

[275] Cited in ibid., 220. Latrobe, in addition to being a lawyer, was the inventor of the Baltimore Heater, a coal-fired parlor heater made of cast iron and fitting into fireplaces as an insert. Also a president of the American Colonization Society, Latrobe had once served as lawyer for Carroll, and, like the Signer, had served on the Maryland Legislature.

made guest of honor in numerous parades. Baltimore was one of the cities that played host to the European visitor, and Carroll's participation was duly noted in the national press. After New York and Philadelphia, he landed at Baltimore on October 7, and Carroll and other dignitaries were there to meet him:

> The meeting of Lafayette with the venerable Charles Carroll, col. Howard, generals Steuart, Stricker, Reed, Benson, and other revolutionary soldiers in the *tent of Washington*, had a most powerful effect on the feelings of all ... He grasped their hands, he folded them in his arms, and, with his eyes brimful of tears, and others who, like him, had fairly stood in the hottest of the fight in many battles, were dissolved by the pressure of the recollections that thickened upon them.[276]

Charles Carroll and his wife Molly had hosted the Marquis at dinner many years previous, and one of the Signer's biographers noted that, "the passage of time had made less formidable the twenty years' difference between their ages, and Lafayette's mind was no longer that of an immature boy who had found it romantic to enlist for American liberty." At the same time, Carroll was "proud to be the friend of this man who had opposed the violence of the Jacobins."[277]

The same year, a presidential election was held to determine who would succeed James Monroe and become the nation's sixth president. Five candidates presented themselves: John Quincy Adams, son of the second President, a former Federalist who had become a National Republican, and who held affiliations with other political parties throughout his

[276] *Niles Weekly Register,* October 16, 1824, cited in Smith, 293.
[277] Smith, 292.

career; Andrew Jackson, a noted war hero from the Battle of New Orleans in 1815; Henry Clay, the "sage of Ashland"; William H. Crawford of Georgia; and John C. Calhoun of South Carolina, who withdrew early and sought the vice presidency, to which he was elected.[278] Jackson, a staunch Democrat, represented a totally new breed of politics, in which the common man found a home; Quincy Adams, on the other hand, represented an older aristocratic order growing out of his Federalist tradition. Once the election was completed, no candidate received a majority of electoral votes. The election was thrown into the House of Representatives, where the three leading candidates were Jackson, Adams, and Crawford. Clay, being eliminated, urged his friends to vote for Adams,

[278] Crawford, a Democratic-Republican, served as Secretary of the Treasury under Presidents Madison and Monroe, as well as a U.S. Senator from Georgia. He had been born in Virginia but left there at an early age; nonetheless, many viewed him as one who would continue the Virginia dynasty of Jefferson, Madison, and Monroe. Henry Clay of Kentucky, known as the "sage of Ashland" after the name of his estate in Lexington, who began as a Democratic-Republican, later, because of his political conservativism, a National Republican, and eventually a Whig, was an American statesman of the highest standard. He helped guide a fragile Union through several critical impasses and is best remembered for his initiative in developing and spearheading the Compromise of 1850. Such temporary arrangements, however, could not forestall forever the Union's eventual disruption and the coming of the Civil War. John C. Calhoun, a Southern states' rights Democrat, had begun his career as a political conservative but gradually took positions favorable to nullification, limited government, states' rights, and opposition to high-protective tariffs. He served as Secretary of War under Monroe, was pro-slavery, and spent the last twenty years of his life as a U.S. Senator from South Carolina, working to unite the South against the abolitionists' attacks on slavery.

thus disobeying the instructions of their state legislature to vote for Jackson. Once Adams was elected President and appointed Clay Secretary of State, charges of a corrupt bargain haunted the Kentuckian for the remainder of his career.

Charles Carroll was an indirect player in the campaign. Though a member of a party whose strength had long since gone, Carroll's old allegiances were firm. At least one of his biographers feels this was to his detriment in 1824 because "he had clung to certain principles of the Federalist Party at a time when most of its members were finding it expedient to modify their views," a new political generation was in power, one which "neither remembered nor cared that Mr. Carroll of Carrollton had subscribed to the old Federalist Party."[279] According to one account, Charles Carroll and fellow Marylander Rodger Brooke Taney, who would eventually become the first Catholic Chief Justice of the Supreme Court, both favored the election of Andrew Jackson because, at least in the case of Carroll, he felt the General would have greater respect for, and acquiesce to, the old members of the Federalist establishment, whereas Quincy Adams, who had been a Federalist as a young man but had broken with them (though not with political conservativism), would entirely proscribe the party. Adams was naturally disappointed and recorded in his diary that he had received a visit from Maryland Congressman Henry R. Warfield on February 7, 1825, at which the congressman told Adams he was still uncertain for whom he would cast his ballot. Adams continued his entry:

> I said I regretted much that Mr. Carroll, for whose character I entertained a profound veneration, and Mr. Taney, of whose talents I had heard high encomium,

[279] Smith, 290–291.

> should harbor such opinions of me. I could assure him that I would never be at the head of any administration of proscription to any party—political or geographical. I had differed from the Federal Party on many important occasions, but I had always done justice to the talents and services of the individuals composing it, and to their merits as members of this Union. I had been discarded by the Federal Party upon differences of principle, and I had not separated from one party to make myself the slave of another.[280]

If 1824 was significant, 1826, the fiftieth anniversary of the signing of the Declaration of Independence in Philadelphia, was monumental. By then, Jefferson, John Adams, and Carroll were the only three signers living, and none was able to participate in the observances—the first two because of the ravages of age,[281] and Carroll because he had previously turned down a similar invitation by the city of New York. On August 2, 1826, exactly fifty years to the day Carroll had affixed his signature to the Declaration of Independence, the legendary Daniel Webster of Massachusetts gave an oration praising him at Faneuil Hall, Boston:

> Of the illustrious signers of the Declaration of Independence there now remains only Charles Carroll. He seems an aged oak, standing alone on the plain, which time has spared a little longer after all his contemporaries have been leveled with the dust. Venerable object! We delight to gather around its trunk while it yet stands, and to dwell beneath its shadow. Sole survivor of an assembly of as great men as the world has witnessed, in

[280] Gurn, 226–227. The entry is taken from *The Diary of John Quincy Adams,* edited by Allan Nevins.

[281] Jefferson and John Adams would both die on July 4, 1826.

> a transaction one of the most important that history records, what thoughts, what interesting reflections, must fill his elevated and devout soul! If to dwell on the past, how touching its recollections; if to survey the present, how happy, how joyous, how full of the fruition of that hope which his ardent patriotism indulged; if he glance at the future, how does the prospect of his country's advancement almost bewilder his weakened conception! Fortunate, distinguished patriot! Interesting relic of the past! Let him know that while we honor the dead we do not forget the living, and that there is not a heart here that does not fervently pray that heaven may keep him yet back from the society of his companions.[282]

Carroll may have been the last of the signers, but he was a man who seemed to remain perpetually young. One of his biographers noted that people much younger than he "found that he was only too glad to meet them on their own level, and perfectly able to do so."[283] In the fiftieth year after his signing of America's foundational document, Congress, quite unusually, invited the Catholic Bishop of Charleston, John England, to address the body—the Protestant chaplain having ceded him his place. Bishop England, an immigrant from the Cork City and a priest of the Diocese of Cork, Ireland, came to America's southland a few years earlier as bishop of a diocese which included both Georgia and both Carolinas. In a short time he had made quite a name nationally and achieved a great deal,[284] especially in his dealings with non-Catholics; he had preached in several Protestant pulpits, created a unique system of church governance with his bicameral body of

[282] Cited in Gurn, 240–241.
[283] Smith, 304.
[284] Gurn, 234.

Vestry (corresponding to the U.S. Senate) and House of Lay Delegates (corresponding to the U.S. House of Representatives), had begun the first Catholic newspaper in the new nation—the *United States Catholic Miscellany*, had founded a school for free Black children, and was held in particularly high regard by so many of his fellow Americans. On this occasion, he answered accusations against his Church—particularly that she was aristocratic, if not despotic in her principles, not suited for the type of government created in America, and her spirit was opposed to republicanism. In answering these objections, he pointed to several world situations which refuted such claims, and, in his own land he rhetorically asked the question: "What was the religion of Charles Carroll of Carrollton? Men who make such assertions cannot have read our Declaration of Independence."

People were continually taken aback by the sprightliness of Charles Carroll in his advancing years. One such was the prominent American Josiah Quincy who had a quite lengthy visit with him in 1826.[285]

> I paid two visits to Charles Carroll (the signer of the Declaration of Independence), and dined with him and Mr. Gallatin at Mr. Caton's, where the service, though the most elegant I had ever seen, in no wise eclipsed the conversation ... Old Mr. Carroll, courtly in manners and bright in mind, was the life of the party. He was then in his ninetieth year, but carried himself as if thirty years younger than his contemporary, John Adams. I have never seen an old man so

[285] Josiah Quincy (1772–1864) was an American educator and political figure; a member of the U.S. House of Representatives, a mayor of Boston, a president of Harvard, and, along with Charles Carroll, a member of the Federalist Party.

> absolutely unconscious of his age. One reason may have been that Carroll was very spare in his person, and had no surplus pound of mortality to weigh down the spirit. On terminating my first call on this very active patriarch, he started from the chair, ran downstairs before me, and opened the front door ... Aghast at this unexpected proceeding, I began to murmur my regrets and mortification in causing him the exertion ... Exertion! exclaimed Mr. Carroll. Why, what do you take me for? I have ridden sixteen miles on horseback this morning, and am good for as much more this afternoon.[286]

On his eighty-ninth birthday, a significant celebration was given him, and one publication took note of it:

> It was highly gratifying to see the last surviving signer of the Declaration of Independence passing into his *ninetieth* year still exhibiting so perfect a model of elegant manners, such a happy example of cheerfulness and intellectual refinement, erect and sprightly as any of the party; left, as it would seem, by Providence to inculcate by their visible fruits the inestimable value of temperance, cleanliness, regularity in diet, and bodily and religious exercises, and a wise government of the grosser passions. He plunges into his limestone spring bath every morning before sunrise, and still rides on horseback with pleasure, in good weather. A large portion of the day is devoted to reading. Having received at St. Omer's the

[286] Cited in Smith, 298. Albert Gallatin was a one-time Secretary of the Treasury under Jefferson. Ellen Hart Smith also notes that, contrary to Quincy's statement, Carroll was then in his eighty-ninth year.

> best classical education, he has always retained his partiality for Latin and French literature.[287]

Philip Hone, the famed American Diarist and one-time Mayor of New York City, paid two visits to Charles Carroll in his later years. On the first occasion, Hone admitted it was a visit "which I have long been wishing for." Hone remarked of Carroll, then into his nineties:

> His faculties are very little impaired, except his sight, which within the last few months has failed a little, and deprived him of the pleasure of reading at all times, which he has heretofore enjoyed. He is gay, cheerful, political and talkative. He described to me his manner of living: He takes a cold bath every morning in the summer, plunging headlong into it; rides on horseback from eight to twelve miles; drinks water at dinner; has never drunk spirituous liquors at any period of his life, but drinks a glass or two of madeira wine every day, and sometimes champagne and claret; takes as much exercise as possible; goes to bed at nine o'clock, and rises before day.[288]

The issue of Catholic emancipation in Ireland was an issue on the minds of many on both sides of the Atlantic in the late 1820s. Britain had passed a number of Catholic Relief Acts in

[287] *The American Farmer*, September 22, 1826, quoted in *Niles Weekly Register*, September 30, 1826, cited in Gurn, 247–248.

[288] Bayard Tuckerman (ed.), *The Diary of Philip Hone,* cited in ibid., 264. Philip Hone (1780–1851) was also the first President of the Delaware and Hudson Canal Company in 1825 and 1826. Its purpose was the transport of coal from the anthracite coal regions of Northeastern Pennsylvania by canal boats to points north and south on the Hudson River; north to Kingston, New York, and south to New York City, thus providing coal fuel to large portions of the country. The town of Honesdale, Pennsylvania, bears his name.

the late eighteenth century, but much was left to be done for Catholics; the right to hold senior government offices, to be members of the Privy Council, to hold judgeships, or to sit in Parliament were still denied them. Petitions to remove such restrictions were defeated by large parliamentary majorities in the early eighteenth century, and an emancipation bill failed in 1819, but two years later a further measure passed the House of Commons; the political argument seemed to have won, but much opposition still remained in the House of Lords and with the monarch, George IV. In 1823, the establishment of the Catholic Association began a new phase of development and created a momentum that was added to by the press and the work of Catholic clergy who played a vital role as local organizers and channels of information throughout Ireland. The resounding victory of Daniel O'Connell, long since titled Ireland's Liberator, in an 1827 election in County Clare, in which he defeated the candidate of the government party, convinced the home government in London that Catholic emancipation could not be delayed any longer. Such became a reality in April, 1829.[289]

The movement for Irish emancipation attracted large numbers of supporters in the United States, among those of Irish descent and others. Especially conspicuous was George Washington Parke Custis, the adopted son of the nation's first president. Custis headed an organization called The Friends of the Civil and Religious Liberty of Ireland in the District of Columbia. Apparently his interest was not merely perfunctory; rather, "he worked with intense zeal, animated by the recollection of the part played by Ireland and her sons

[289] For a further treatment of the issue, see S. J. Connolly, (ed.), *The Oxford Companion to Irish History* (Oxford University Press, 1998), 75.

in the War of Independence."[290] Charles Carroll's ancestry was both English and Irish, Catholic on both sides, and though his life was by now far removed from that of Charles Carroll the Settler, he always retained his love for the land of his ancestors. Custis had written a highly laudatory letter to the Signer, soliciting a donation for the cause, and Carroll promptly responded that a similar organization for the relief of Irish Roman Catholics had been formed in the city of Baltimore, of which he was a member, and he felt it somewhat inappropriate to send yet another contribution to the same organization in another area. At the same time, he wanted Custis to know his true feelings of the larger matter:

> When I signed the Declaration of Independence I had in view not only our independence of England but the toleration of all sects professing the Christian religion and communicating to them all equal rights. Happily this wise and salutary measure has taken place for eradicating religious feuds and persecution, and becomes a useful lesson to all governments. Reflecting, as you must, on the disabilities, I may truly say, of the proscription of the Roman Catholics in Maryland, you will not be surprised that I had much at heart this grand design founded on mutual charity, the basis of our holy religion.[291]

While rumor had it, in 1824, that Carroll had favored the election of Andrew Jackson, in hopes his attitude toward aging Federalists would be benign, when the hero of the Battle of New Orleans was elected in the election of 1828,

[290] Gurn, 259.

[291] Charles Carrollton to George Washington Parke Custis, February 20, 1829, in the *Truth Teller*, February 28, 1829, cited in ibid., 261.

Carroll appears to have stayed out of the fray. He was quite clear, in correspondence to an interested inquirer, that he took "no part in the contest respecting the election of the next President," adding that, "I give no opinion which of the candidates should be the choice of the people … my only wish is that it may fall on him whose measures will be solely directed to the public good."[292] The same year did, however, witness his public appearance at an event of enormous historical importance, the laying of the foundation stone of the Baltimore and Ohio Railroad. The great significance lay in the fact of a man of ninety years, who had known life in Colonial America, and was present to witness the groundbreaking of an enterprise which, in a few brief years, in company with numerous other railroads, totally transformed the face of the country.

> The Signer threw all his prestige behind the Baltimore and Ohio Railroad, or B&O. At age ninety, he chaired a committee to petition the Assembly on behalf of the railroad, and then he served on its board of directors. The project fit Carrollton's political ideas as well as his business interests. He thought government should support private projects that promoted the common good, without creating bureaucratic programs. With the railroad, Carroll believed, Baltimore would become "one of the largest and commercial cities in the United States" within fifty years.[293]

[292] *Niles Weekly Register*, June 2, 1827, cited in ibid., 254.

[293] Charles Carroll of Carrollton to Lady Stafford, February 26, 1828, in Field, 210–211, cited in McDermott, 245. The public event took place in Baltimore on July 4, 1828, and Carroll regarded it as "second only to his signing the Declaration of Independence," Gurn, 256.

The following year, the First Provincial Council of the Roman Catholic Church met in the city of Baltimore, the premier see in the United States. Liverpool-born James Whitfield was by now Archbishop of Baltimore, the only native-born Englishman to occupy the see. Numerous decrees were passed on such topics as uniformity in the administration of the sacraments, priestly conduct, Catholic publications, schools for the young, and so forth. Its significance lay in the fact of its being the first such gathering of proportion since the establishment of the American hierarchy in 1789.[294] At its conclusion, the Archbishop, in company with all the attending prelates, paid a visit to Charles Carroll at his manor house:

> He received the prelates with his accustomed courtesy and grace; and he was much rejoiced, when now so near the close of his mortal career, to see that the Church which he loved was so visibly keeping pace with the rapid movements of the country.[295]

The Council had received significant press coverage. The *Baltimore Gazette*, in particular, focused on the visit of the Catholic bishops to the Signer:

> Pursuant to a resolution of the prelates who composed the council, they went in a body on Tuesday, the 20th instant, to pay their respects to the venerable Charles Carroll of Carrollton, as the surviving signer of the glorious Charter of the country's freedom, and one of the most aged and exemplary members of their Church. They were most hospitably

[294] Spalding, 103.
[295] Gurn, 263.

> entertained and delighted with the good old patriot and his amiable family.[296]

Still another account of Carroll in his final years comes from an English author, James Boardman. In his work, *America and the Americans*, this non-Catholic writer had occasion to attend Mass in the Baltimore Basilica of the Assumption:

> The service was conducted with considerable splendor, aided by most delicious music; and the sermon, like almost all I have had the pleasure of hearing from the pulpits of the Church of Rome, inculcated good works and contained no uncharitable allusions to those who professed a different creed. The crowded congregation consisted chiefly of Irish, of which nation there are great numbers in Baltimore. Among the assembled throng in this holy place one individual in particular arrested our attention from the moment of his entrance. It was the venerable Charles Carroll, the last survivor of that patriot band who pledged "their lives, their fortunes, and their sacred honor" to establish the liberties of their country. This highly regarded gentleman ... was then in his ninety-second year, yet walked along the isle with a vigorous step.[297]

After a life of great dissipation and a giving up of the Faith, Charles Carroll of Homewood, the Signer's son had died in 1825. Though undoubtedly full of the sorrow of any father burying his son, Carroll wrote to his daughter-in-law, Harriet Chew Carroll, "I presume that he expressed anguish and repentance for the life he led," the Signer prayed, "the course

[296] *Baltimore Gazette*, cited in *Niles Weekly Register*, October 31, 1829, cited in ibid., 263.

[297] Ibid., 263–264.

of which both of us have more cause to lament than his end. He has appeared before a judge, the Searcher of Hearts, and most merciful; let us pray that he has found mercy at that dread Tribunal."[298] Earlier the same year, Carroll's son-in-law, Robert Goodloe Harper, to whom he was very close, died suddenly one morning following breakfast; "I have lost a son-in-law whom I loved and esteemed," he lamented.[299]

Carroll had always supported the Church materially; such was manifested in his bequests to St. Charles Seminary in Catonsville, just across the road from his manor house. He gave land adjacent to his home in Annapolis for the building of St. Mary's Church, as well as the land adjacent to Carrollton Manor in Buckeystown for the building of St. Joseph's Church. He also funded Catholic orphanages and contributed to a

[298] Charles Carroll of Carrollton to Harriet Chew Carroll, April 12, 1825, cited in McDermott, 247. It is McDermott's opinion that Carroll had not given his children sufficient discipline, perhaps because of his frequent absences from home. He was an emotionally reserved man, which somewhat deprived his children of the affirmation he might have offered if more outgoing. Such is not to suggest that Carroll of Homewood bore no responsibility for his own life; he was overly concerned with his eventual inheritance and might have forgiven his father for his possible defects, but, as McDermott notes, "deprived of the sacraments, and alienated from religion, Homewood had little incentive to leave his resentments behind." Carroll would not allow his son to be buried in the chapel of Doughoregan Manor but in the family graveyard a few miles from Annapolis. He remained close to his daughter-in-law, Harriet, and she expressed her willingness to move to Maryland. The patriarch, however, while seeing to her financial welfare, felt she should remain in Philadelphia, where her daughters would have a better chance of entering into good marriages. See ibid., 247–248.

[299] Charles Carroll of Carrollton to William Gibbons, January 15, 1825, cited in ibid., 247.

school for the education of poor children. An interesting episode occurred, too, in the case of a Kentucky seminarian named Martin J. Spalding. Coming from a generations-old English Catholic family who had emigrated from Southern Maryland to Kentucky in the eighteenth century, Martin had completed his initial seminary studies in Bardstown, Kentucky, and was being sent to Rome to complete his theology. He wrote from Baltimore to a former priest-teacher, before sailing for the Eternal City, that, "among other privileges we have had the pleasure of seeing the venerable patriot, Charles Carroll, the last of our Revolutionary heroes. Though ninety-three years of age he is quite vigorous and remarkably cheerful. He is still able, he says, to mount his horse and ride six or seven miles without great fatigue. It is a source of gratification to us to have received the good will and benediction of the venerable patriot just on the eve of our leaving our native land."[300] Curiously, Spalding was to become Archbishop of Baltimore in 1864.

Splendid recollections of the final years of Carroll's life have been left by his close friend, Fr. Charles Constantine Pise. The priest noted of his old friend that he had often "seen him … spending his summers under the shade of those trees which his father's hand had planted nearly a century and a half ago, and which … love to twine their hospitable boughs over the venerable manor of 'Doughoregan.'" Pise felt Carroll's memories of the American Revolution were among his favorite to recall:

> It was deeply riveted in his recollection, with all its details and all its dangers; often I have heard him tell,

[300] The letter, written to a Fr. Byrne, was reproduced in John Lancaster Spalding's biography of his uncle, *Life of the Most Reverend M. J. Spalding,* cited in Gurn, 265.

> with an eye flashing with enthusiasm, of the destitute state of the country, of the want of troops, of discipline, of ammunition, of everything, when the first Congress declared the colonies independent. The members of that Congress were all fresh in his memory. He would often describe the persons and characters of the leading personages of those days, and passages of their speeches which had then made an impression on his mind, he still remembered. "Were I to enter the hall at this remote period," I once heard him say, "and meet my associates who signed the instrument of our independence, I would know them all, from Hancock down to Stephen Hopkins."

Adding a further recollection of Carroll's intellectual proclivities:

> I once entered his study and found him intently absorbed in meditating the treatise of Cicero on old age. He entered on a highly entertaining and critical discussion on the subject of the philosophic writings of that extraordinary Roman. He seemed to turn with inexpressible satisfaction to some passages of the treatise he was pursuing; and dwelt with a deep feeling of the wisdom of it.

And on his priorities, religious and political: "After the Bible," he added, with his peculiar earnestness and vivacity of manner, "and the *Following of Christ*, give me, Sir, the philosophic works of Cicero."[301]

The presidential election of 1832, which resounded in an overwhelming reelection victory for President Andrew Jackson, nonetheless was a three-way fight, with the National Republicans

[301] Rowland, 11, 363–365.

(soon to be Whigs) nominating Henry Clay, Carroll's old friend. A third, the Anti-Masonic Party, also put forward a candidate, though from the outset there was little doubt about the outcome. A group of young National Republican men held a convention in Baltimore in May of that year, and at that convention, a committee was selected to pay a visit to Charles Carroll, by then living with the Catons at Front and Lombard Streets in Baltimore. Carroll was apparently deeply moved by the tributes rendered him,[302] and he "seemed to give Clay his blessing when he received ... [them] at his home."[303] Shortly thereafter, he confided to Fr. Pise, when the latter visited him, "you find me very low ... I am going, Sir, to the tomb of my fathers."[304] Though Carroll was full aware of his condition and his advanced age, the slowing down apparently came on him rather quickly. Just weeks before, in the spring of 1832, Philip Hone had revisited Baltimore and had seen Carroll for the second time. The Signer was able to ride around Baltimore with him on horseback, visit Doughoregan Manor and at least one other country seat, and, though still very sprightly, Hone could see that he had aged:

> Mr. and Mrs. Caton having called this morning to invite us, we passed an hour or two delightfully at their house in the evening. The family were all present. Mr. Carroll was cheerful and talkative, and enjoyed himself very much until nine o'clock, when, according to his uniform practice, he took the arm of Mrs. MacTavish, and quietly left the room. I feel while in the presence of this venerable man as if I were permitted to converse

[302] *Niles Weekly Register,* May 26, 1832, gave extensive coverage to the meeting; see Gurn, 266–268.

[303] McDermott, 258.

[304] Ibid.

with one of the patriarchs, revisiting the land which, in days long gone, he had enriched with his patriotic counsels. He is in his ninety-sixth year; his hearing is defective, and his memory of recent events imperfect, but he presents a beautiful example of the close of a well-spent life—serene, cheerful, and happy; prepared, it would seem, "to take his rest, with all his country's blest." It is very probable I shall never see him again after the present visit, and this reflection enhanced the value of the delightful hour I have just passed in his company. I made Mary take a seat by his side, and she has it to say that she conversed some time with the last surviving signer of the immortal Declaration of Independence.[305]

[305] Smith, 309–310. Hone's reference to Mary is his daughter Mary (Hone) Schermerhorn.

CHAPTER 6

THE END AND THE LEGACY

Five years before his death, Charles Carroll expressed sentiments which much summed up his life:

> To obtain religious, as well as civil liberty, I entered zealously into the Revolution, and observing the Christian religion divided into many sects, I founded the hope that no one would be so predominant as to become the religion of the State. That hope was thus early entertained, because all of them joined in the same cause, with few exceptions of individuals. God grant that this religious liberty may be preserved in these States, to the end of time, and that all believing in the religion of Christ may practice the leading principle of charity, the basis of every virtue.[306]

That life was now waning, especially during the year 1832. He had been in the habit of spending winters with his daughter and son-in-law, Mary and Richard Caton, in Baltimore. By the time he reached his ninety-fifth birthday, he had

[306] Charles Carroll of Carrollton to Rev. John Standford, October 9, 1827, cited in Rowland, 11, 358. Standford was Chaplain of Humane and Criminal Institutions in the city of New York.

become terribly feeble, weighed less than one hundred pounds, but his spirit was vibrant until the end. His daughter shared nursing tasks with her daughter, Emily MacTavish, the one Caton daughter who had not settled in Europe and with whom Carroll was particularly close. His physician was Dr. Richard Steuart, whose family had been long-time friends of the Carrolls in Annapolis; the doctor came each day to check on the Signer, but little could be done medically—old age will always be just that. Steuart was joined by other doctors who cared for Carroll and whom Carroll often jokingly referred to as his "Aesculapiuses."[307] The scene of his reception of the Sacrament of Anointing, or, as called in his time, Extreme Unction, has been captured in fine detail:

> Old Mr. Carroll had been placed in a large easy-chair; before him the blessed candles, a crucifix, and a silver bowl of holy water stood on a little table. A daughter and grandchildren knelt on either side of his chair. Doctor Steuart, kneeling too out of courtesy,[308] was profoundly impressed by the scene: "The ceremony proceeded. The old gentleman had been for a long time suffering from weak eyes, and could not endure the proximity of the lights immediately before him. His eyes were three-fourths kept closed but he was so familiar with the forms of this solemn ceremony that he responded and acted as if he saw everything passing around. At the moment of offering the Host[309] he leaned forward without opening his eyes, yet responsive

[307] Aesculapius was a hero and god of medicine in Greek mythology. This was specifically referred to in the *Oration in Honor of the Late Charles Carroll of Carrollton before the Philodemic Society of Georgetown College*, December 13, 1832, cited in Smith, 310.

[308] Steuart was a non-Catholic.

[309] Holy Viaticum.

> to the word of the administration of the Holy Offering. It was done with so much intelligence and grace that no one could doubt for a moment how fully his soul was alive to the act.
>
> The rites completed and tears wiped away from black faces as well as white—for Mr. Carroll had been as kind a master as a father—his physician suggested that he take a little nourishment, for he had been fasting all day. 'Thank you, Doctor, not just now,' Charles Carroll answered him gently, 'this ceremony is so deeply interesting to the Christian that it supplies all the wants of nature. I feel no desire for food.' "[310]

He was later placed in bed, continued to refuse food, and, appearing to be lying in an uncomfortable position, his granddaughter asked the physician to move him a bit. "Thank you, Doctor," was his response; he fell into a deep sleep, and sometime after midnight, he entered eternity. It was November 14, 1832.

"He met his end like a philosopher and a Christian," his old friend Fr. Charles Constantine Pise said of him, and upon seeing the dying patriot very shortly before death, and listening to the sentiments he expressed, the priest was enormously impressed with his "earnest expression … calm resignation … amiable conviction," believing all of them displayed "his character as a philosopher as much perhaps as any act or saying of his past life."[311]

Fr. Pise once recalled that Carroll's attachment to his Catholic Faith was "firm and unchanging," that he was a

[310] Smith, 311. Fr. John C. Chaunce, President of St. Mary's College, administered the last rites to the Signer. He later became the first Bishop of Natchez, Mississippi.

[311] Cited in Gurn, 275.

Catholic "not merely by birth ... but by a thorough investigation into religious matters." He felt him, because of his advance education, an "enlightened Christian," though his Catholicism was something he very much put into practice.

> He confessed and received Communion monthly, attended Mass every Sunday and holyday of obligation, observed all the minutest rules and customs of the Church. He was first on every good work, first to subscribe to the relief of the poor, the education of the orphan, the erection of churches; first to appear on Good Friday at the ceremony of kissing the Cross; first to receive the ashes on Ash Wednesday, and first to receive the psalms on Palm Sunday. And all this he performed with the utmost simplicity and humility, perfectly removed from anything like show or ostentation.[312]

His death, as one might expect, was an event of national interest. Newspapers throughout the country were replete with eulogistic literature, and even the nation's president, Andrew Jackson, sent a communique observing that "no one estimated higher than I did his claims, whilst living, upon the gratitude and love of his country; none will cherish more sacredly his memory now that he is taken from us by the Great Disposer of the affairs of this world."[313] His funeral took place on

[312] Ibid., 287.

[313] *National Gazette*, November 20, 1832, cited in ibid., 281. Jackson sincerely regretted not being able to attend the Signer's funeral, but events of the Nullification Crisis in South Carolina demanded his presence in Washington. Just days before the funeral, the state had announced all federal tariffs null, void, and nonbinding in the state. It was one of the major events underscoring sectional differences of constitutional interpretation and has always been considered an early indicator of the issues which would divide the country and lead to the war between the states in 1861.

November 17, 1832, a day marred by heavy rain in the city of Baltimore. The Solemn Requiem Mass was offered in the Basilica of the Assumption by Archbishop James Whitfield, the pallbearers were: Dr. James Stewart, William Lorman, Jeremiah Hoffman, William Patterson, Robert Oliver, and Robert Barry.[314] Officials in attendance included the Mayor of the City of Baltimore, the Governor of Maryland, members of the President's cabinet (headed by the Vice President, John C. Calhoun), United States Senators and Representatives, Executive Council of Maryland, President and Directors of the Baltimore and Ohio Railroad, members of the diplomatic corps, and numerous patriotic and military groups, along with countless Baltimoreans and citizens who had come from many parts of the country to pay their respects. The diary of Sulpician Fr. Louis Regis Deloul provides interesting details:

> Body was removed from the house at 9:30 A.M. Father Piot, in Black dalmatic, carried the cross, with Fathers A. J. Elder and Lhomme in Copes; Fathers Joubert (deacon) and Roger Smith in Dalmatics. There was a grand procession from near Market Street and Charles by a crowd that was immense but peaceful. We all wore surplice and biretta; I was in cope between the deacon and subdeacon. I began Matins at the entrance of Mr. Caton's house and finished Nones at the upper end of Charles Street. Father Cranche was Master of ceremonies; Fathers Tessier and deBarth waited at the Archbishop's; Father White was somewhere or other; Father Pise was at the organ; Father Jamison was at his own affairs; all the rest of the clergy were in the procession; and

[314] It is not clear if the Stewart whom Gurn lists as a pallbearer is the same doctor who served as Carroll's physician; if so, the first name, and the spelling of the surname, do not coincide.

> Father Damphoux was there in clerical cape. The flag, draped in crepe, was carried in front of the corpse and in behind the cross. All those in surplice walked ahead of the body, all those in cope or dalmatic after. The Archbishop [James Whitfield] received the procession at the door of the Cathedral; he sang the high Mass. I served him as assistant priest; Father Eccleston preached quite well (though another source reports "no funeral oration"). When the Mass ended the Archbishop went to have breakfast, and I conducted the absolution. The procession was supposed to resume and go as far as Cove Street, but the rain prevented it. The carriages picked us up near the Cathedral at 12:30, and we arrived at the Manor at 4:30. It rained the whole time; there was a score of carriages with the Archbishop and seven priests. Mr. Carroll was buried in a vault which he had prepared for himself under the spot where he had been accustomed to pray in his chapel, on the Gospel side, quite near the altar.[315]

A further diary entry dealing with the after-funeral luncheon at Doughoregan Manor is quite humorous:

> During the meal which began at 5:15, Mr. Hammond, a neighbor, had overindulged *[pres de liqueur]*; he got up and cursed everyone, especially the Archbishop. Someone shut him up, but after the meal he began again. Mr. Hollingsworth tried to calm him down but didn't succeed. Then Mr. George Howard, the present Governor of Maryland, grabbed hold of him, dragged him to the porch in the hall, shoved him to the ground and fell

[315] Charles P. Connor, "Great Events in United States Catholic History in the Baltimore Basilica," (Baltimore: Unpublished Paper, 2017), 7.

> on him with a crash. Hammond was carried off ... the Governor came back to speak to Colonel Moore and me; he told us "I settled him." "Yes, Governor (I answered him), it appears you can rule both with your heart and with your fist." Father Chanche left about 6:00 with the Archbishop. I left with Fathers Lhomme and Randanne and Mr. Digges at 7:00 and arrived back at 9:45. Father Elder and Father Verot and Mr. Lesne left at 8:00 and arrived at midnight. It was very dark and rainy.[316]

One biographer of Carroll has noted that the north wing of Doughoregan Manor is formed by the oldest private chapel in the United States. The description of the Signer's final monument underscores the author's point of Charles Carroll's being a strict Catholic:

> On the north wall of the chapel, and to the right of the altar, there is an entablature by Bartholomew. A pen rests upon the Declaration of Independence, the thirteen stars of the original states above, and over all a cross.[317]

One could only imagine the tributes from around the country which were expressed upon learning of the Signer's death. One such example, reflective of so many others, was that of Robert Walsh, editor of the *National Gazette* in Philadelphia. A conservative Federalist much like Charles Carroll, as well as a strong Catholic, Walsh reminisced about visiting Doughoregan often as a child; he described Carroll as a man of refinement and the highest courtesy, one whose patriotism "never lost its earnestness and elevation," one in whom the absence of "all pretension, egotism, *hauteur,* severity, formed

[316] Ibid., 7–8.

[317] Gurn, 283. The memorial was executed in Rome in 1853 and was erected by Colonel Charles Carroll, the Signer's grandson.

as remarkable a characteristic as the lively and constant presence of his mind for all persons and concerns in any relation of fellowship."[318]

Such tributes became commonplace among observers of Carroll's contributions, as well as early biographers. His positive accomplishments for his country were also not lost on generations who followed him. Early in the twentieth century, statues of himself and his fellow Marylander John Hanson were officially received into Statuary Hall in Congress. At the time, presentations were made by members of the Senate and House of Representatives. An especially interesting one regarding Carroll came from a senator from Massachusetts, George F. Hoar. He had come to the Senate in 1877 and served until his death in 1904, one year after the statues were placed. Hoar was a Harvard graduate, as well as from Harvard Law School, and had joined the Free Soil Party, later becoming a Republican at that group's inception in the 1850s. He was an abolitionist, strictly convinced of the immorality of slavery, and staunchly opposed to the Democratic Party as representative of the "saloon keeper, ballot box stuffer, and Ku Klux Klan."[319] He was a man opposed to political corruption and strongly favored the rights of African and Native Americans. He was also an economic nationalist who saw capitalism as true progress for civilization and favored high-protective tariffs to protect American industries from foreign competition. Given his comments at the reception of Charles Carroll's statue, his background is significant.

[318] Cited in ibid., 289.

[319] Such description appears in Wikipedia's biography of Hoar, whose middle name, Frisbie, was the name by which most of his contemporaries knew him.

He noted that Carroll was a devoted Catholic, a member of that Church "which preserved for mankind religion, learning, literature, and law through the gloomy centuries known as the dark Ages." His comments became even more realistic:

> Yet it is the only denomination of Christians against which anything of theological bitterness or bigotry seems to have survived amid the liberality of our enlightened day. Every few years we hear of secret societies, and even political parties, organized with the sole view of excluding the members of a single Christian church from their equal privileges as American citizens. Yet certainly the men of the Catholic faith have never been behind their countrymen, either as patriot citizens or as patriot soldiers. This spirit of bigotry would have denied the ordinary rights of Americans not only to Charles Carroll and his illustrious cousins, the Archbishop, to Daniel Carroll and to Thomas Fitzsimmons who were among the framers of the Constitution, but to ... Phil Sheridan.[320]

Hoar went on to stress that the American Catholic "in the early days, laid the State which he founded on the eternal principle of religious toleration." Hoar strongly felt the American people, especially the large numbers easily given to anti-Catholic prejudice, should note carefully the positive contributions of the members of the Church of Rome, adding, in the end, that the American Catholic "did his full and

[320] *Proceedings in the Senate and House of Representatives Upon the Reception and Acceptance from the State of Maryland of the Statues of Charles Carroll of Carrollton and of John Hanson, Erected in Statuary Hall of the Capitol*, (Washington: Government Printing Office, 1903), 27–28.

noble share in winning the liberty and in framing the Constitution of the country which he loves as we do and which we love as he does."[321]

Such sentiments found expression in the twentieth century, in 1937, when large religious and civic celebrations were held in memory of the bicentenary of Carroll's birth in 1737. One such gathering was in Baltimore, and Major General Clinton L. Riggs, Adjutant General of the Maryland National Guard and chairman of the commission heading the celebration, received a letter from then-President of the United States, Franklin D. Roosevelt, expressing his regret at not being able to attend. Roosevelt nonetheless desired to join in the tribute "a grateful nation is paying to his life

[321] Ibid., 29. Another comment worth remembering came from the House of Representatives, from Congressman John Dalzell of Pennsylvania. A Republican representing his hometown of Pittsburgh, he was held in very high esteem by Presidents Benjamin Harrison, William McKinley, and Theodore Roosevelt. He spoke upon the reception of Carroll's statue in 1903, saying of the Signer, "He was an enthusiastic Roman Catholic, faithful to the teachings of his church and observant of its customs and obligations. A scholar, a statesman, a man of affairs, a Christian gentleman, he was idolized by his fellow-citizens, not only for what he had done, but for what he was in himself and by way of example to others," ibid., 102. Referring to the anti-Catholic bigotry leveled against him, Carroll's fellow Marylander, Congressman George Pearre, a Republican from the state's 6th congressional district, looked back at the Signer's quarrel with Daniel Dulaney and testified that, "During this written debate he was taunted as 'Jesuit,' 'anti-Christ,' a 'man without a country'; and yet his devotion to the people's cause rose supreme over every insult, over all injustice, and inspired him with an eloquence of diction and a forcefulness of statement which put to rout the great Daniel Dulaney, the peer of any lawyer of his time in England or America," ibid., 86.

and manifold public services." The President described Carroll as one who stands as "one of the notable figures in our history," a man whose "life was as full as his years were long." Roosevelt saw the Signer as a political writer who "could hold his own with the best in the eighteenth century, a century which was supreme in that branch of the literary art." Specifically related to Carroll's own polemics, FDR felt they were "influential in aligning Maryland with the cause of the Revolution." Finally, notice was given that his private life was "adorned by the Christian virtues of fortitude, fidelity, and the integrity which shed luster upon his public service."[322]

In the end, the Catholic Signer from Maryland had achieved much, contributed much, reaped much. He was well recognized by his contemporaries and those of generations after him. In the end, however, the cross atop his monument in St. Mary's Chapel, Doughoregan Manor, speaks it all. His greatest satisfaction had indeed been found in the practice of his Catholic Faith. In an age when heroes are needed, we Catholics surely possess one in this eminent son of Maryland.

[322] Scarff, 50.

BIBLIOGRAPHY

La Chapelle des Jésuites de Saint-Omer. La Fondation Saint-Omer Valeurs Transatlantiques, undated.

La Famille Carroll: Itinéraire du Maryland à Saint-Omer. Steenvoorde: Nord'Imprim, undated.

Proceedings in the Senate and House of Representatives Upon the Reception and Acceptance from the State of Maryland of the Statues of Charles Carroll of Carrollton and of John Hanson, Erected in Statuary Hall of the Capitol. Washington, DC: Government Printing Office, 1903.

Saint-Omer: Musées, Monuments. Promenades. Saint-Omer: Centre des Monuments Nationaux, 2011.

Alden, John Richard. *The American Revolution: 1775–1783*. New York: Harper & Row, 1962.

Andrews, Charles M. *Colonial Background of the American Revolution*. New Haven: Yale University Press, 1924.

Andrews, Wayne (ed.). *Concise Dictionary of American History*. New York: Charles Scribner's Sons, 1962.

Bailyn, Bernard. *The Ideological Origins of the American Revolution*. Cambridge: Harvard University Press, 1967.

Basset, Bernard, S.J. *The English Jesuits: From Campion to Martindale*. New York: Herder & Herder, 1968.

Birzer, Bradley J. *American Cicero: The Life of Charles Carroll*. Wilmington, Delaware: ISI Books, 2010.

Boatner, Mark M. *Encyclopedia of the American Revolution*. New York: David McKay Company, Inc., 1966.

Boyer, Paul S. (ed.). *The Oxford Companion to United States History.* Oxford University Press, 2001.

Brugger, Robert J. *Maryland: A Middle Temperament: 1634–1980.* Baltimore: The Johns Hopkins University Press, 1988.

Carter, Charles Carroll, et al. *Creating Capitol Hill: Place, Proprietors, and People.* Washington, DC: The United States Capitol Historical Society, 2018.

Cervoni, Clarisse. *Lands of Promise: From Saint Omer to Maryland.* Saint-Omer: Les Venterniers, 2015.

Chadwick, H. *St. Omers to Stonyhurst.* London: Burns and Oates, 1962.

Connolly, S. J. (ed.). *The Oxford Companion to Irish History.* Oxford University Press, 1998.

Connor, Charles P. *Pioneer Priests and Makeshift Altars: A History of Catholicism in the Thirteen Colonies.* Irondale, Alabama: EWTN Publishing, 2017.

Cox, Joseph W. *Champion of Southern Federalism: Robert Goodloe Harper of South Carolina.* Port Washington, NY: National University Publications, 1972.

Craven, Wesley Frank. *The Colonies in Transition: 1660–1713.* New York: Harper & Row, 1968.

Curran, Francis X., S.J. *Catholics in Colonial Law.* Chicago: Loyola University Press, 1963.

Curran, Robert Emmett. *Papist Devils: Catholics in British America: 1574–1783.* Washington, DC: The Catholic University of America Press, 2014.

Dawson, Christopher. *The Dividing of Christendom.* New York: Sheed and Ward, 1965.

Ellis, John Tracy. *Catholics in Colonial America.* Baltimore: Helicon, 1965.

Farrelly, Mary Jane. *Anti-Catholicism in America, 1620–1860.* Cambridge University Press, 2018.

———. *Papist Patriots: The Making of an American Catholic Identity.* Oxford University Press, 2012.

Field, Thomas Meagher. *Unpublished Letters of Charles Carroll of Carrollton, and of His Father, Charles Carroll of Doughoregan*. New York: The United States Catholic Historical Society, 1902.

Gipson, Lawrence Henry. *The Coming of the Revolution: 1763–1775*. New York: Harper & Row, 1962.

Grove, William Jarboe. *History of Carrollton Manor, Fredrick County, MD*. Lime Kiln, MD: William J. Grove, 1922.

Guilday, Peter. *The Life and Times of John Carroll: Archbishop of Baltimore: 1735–1815*. New York: The Encyclopedia Press, 1922.

Gurn, Joseph. *Charles Carroll of Carrollton: 1737–1832*. New York: P.J. Kenedy and Sons, 1932.

Hanley, Thomas O'Brien, S.J. *Charles Carroll of Carrollton: The Making of a Revolutionary Gentleman*. Chicago: Loyola University Press, 1982.

———. *Revolutionary Statesman: Charles Carroll and the War*. Chicago: Loyola University Press, 1983.

———. *The American Revolution and Religion*. Washington, DC: The Catholic University of America Press, 1971.

———. *Their Rights & Liberties: The Beginnings of Religious & Political Freedom in Maryland*. Chicago: Loyola University Press, 1984.

Hennesey, James, S.J. *American Catholics*. Oxford University Press, 1981.

Hoffman, Ronald, et al. (eds.). *Dear Papa, Dear Charley: The Papers of Charles Carroll of Carrollton: 1748–1782: Volume II*. Chapel Hill: The University of North Carolina Press, 2001.

———. *Princes of Ireland, Planters of Maryland: A Carroll Saga, 1500–1782*. Chapel Hill: The University of North Carolina Press, 2000.

Hopkins, Joseph G. E. (ed.). *Concise Dictionary of American Biography*. New York: Charles Scribner's Sons, 1964.

Leonard, Lewis A. *Life of Charles Carroll of Carrollton*. New York: Moffat, Yard and Company, 1918.

Livermore, Shaw, Jr. *The Twilight of Federalism: The Disintegration of the Federalist Party: 1815–1830*. Princeton University Press, 1962.

McDermott, Sean. *Charles Carroll of Carrolton: Faithful Revolutionary*. New York: Scepter Publishers, 2002.

Melville, Annabelle M. *John Carroll of Baltimore: Founder of the American Catholic Hierarchy*. New York: Charles Scribner's Sons, 1955.

Metzger, Charles H., S.J. *Catholics and the American Revolution: A Study in Religious Climate*. Chicago: Loyola University Press, 1962.

Miller, John C. *The Federalist Era: 1789–1801*. New York: Harper & Row, 1960.

Morris, Richard B. (ed.). *Encyclopedia of American History*. New York: Harper & Row, 1965.

Parrington, Vernon L. *The Colonial Mind: 1620–1800*. New York: Harcourt Brace and Co., 1954.

Peterman, Thomas J. *Bohemia: 1704–2004: A History of St. Francis Xavier Catholic Shrine in Cecil County, Maryland*. Devon, Pennsylvania: William T. Cooke Publishing, Inc., 2004.

———. *Catholics in Colonial Delmarva*. Devon, Pennsylvania: William T. Cooke Publishing Company, 1996.

Plowden, Charles. *A Short Account of the Establishment of the New See of Baltimore in Maryland and of Consecrating the Right Rev. Dr. John Carroll First Bishop thereof, on the Feast of the Assumption, 1790*. London: J. P. Coghlan, 1790.

Pomfret, John E. *Founding the American Colonies: 1583–1660*. New York: Harper & Row, 1970.

Pratt, Julius W. *A History of United States Foreign Policy*. Englewood Cliffs, NJ: Prentice-Hall, Inc., 1965.

Rowland, Kate Mason. *The Life of Charles Carrollton, 1737–1832, with His Correspondence and Public Papers*. New York: G. P. Putnam's Sons, 1898.

Scarff, John H. (ed.). *The Bicentenary Celebration of the Birth of Charles Carroll of Carrollton: 1737–1837*. Washington, DC: 74th Congress of the United States, 1937.

Semmes, Raphael. *Baltimore as Seen by Visitors: 1783–1860*. Baltimore: Maryland Historical Society, 1953.

Smelser, Marshall. *The Democratic Republic: 1801–1815*. New York: Harper & Row, 1968.

Smith, Ellen Hart. *Charles Carroll Of Carrollton*. New York: Russell & Russell, 1942.

Smith, Goldwin. *A History of England*. New York: Charles Scribner's Sons, 1966.

Spalding, Thomas W. *The Premier See: A History of the Archdiocese of Baltimore, 1789–1989*. Baltimore: The Johns Hopkins University Press, 1989.

Swisher, Carl B. *Roger B. Taney*. Hamden, Connecticut: Archon Books, 1961.

Van Devanter, Ann C. (ed.). *"Anywhere So Long As There Be Freedom": Charles Carroll of Carrollton, His Family & His Maryland*. The Baltimore Museum of Art, 1975.

Wake, Jehanne. *Sisters of Fortune: America's Caton Sisters at Home and Abroad*. New York: Simon & Schuster, 2010.

Weinreb, Ben and Hibbert, Christopher. *The London Encyclopedia*. Macmillan London Limited, 1987.

ABOUT THE AUTHOR

Fr. Charles P. Connor, S.T.L., Ph.D., a priest of the Diocese of Scranton, Pennsylvania, has produced his fourth book for EWTN Publishing, the first three being: *Pioneer Priests and Makeshift Altars: A History of Catholicism in the Thirteen Colonies*, *Faith and Fury: The Rise of Catholicism during the Civil War*, and *Toil and Transcendence: Catholicism in 20th-Century America*. A prolific author, Fr. Connor has also written such works as: *Classic Catholic Converts*, *Defenders of the Faith in Word and Deed*, *The Saint for the Third Millenium: Thérèse of Lisieux*, *Meditations on the Catholic Priesthood*, *The Spiritual Legacy of Archbishop Fulton J. Sheen*, and *John Cardinal O'Connor and the Culture of Life*. He has co-produced dozens of series for EWTN and has actively engaged in preaching retreats for priests, religious, and laity throughout the United States.

Fr. Connor served in his native Diocese for eighteen years and for over a decade as Professor of Systematic Theology and Church History at Mount St. Mary's Seminary in Emmitsburg, Maryland. Fr. Connor holds a B.A. and M.A. in United States history from the University of Scranton, and a Ph.D. in the same discipline from

Fordham University in New York City. Then followed a Ph.B. from the Institute of Philosophy at the Catholic University of Louvain in Belgium, an S.T.B. from the Gregorian University in Rome, an M.A. in theology from the Angelicum University in Rome, and an S.T.L. from the Pontifical John Paul II Institute for Studies on Marriage and Family in Washington, D.C.